Look for the Effin' Rainbows

A SELF-HELP GUIDE

Not really but it will give you a laugh

IRENE WIGNALL

Look for the Effin' Rainbows — A Self-help Guide
By Irene Wignall

ISBN: 978-1-8380993-1-2

Cover Design by Jo Blakeley

Book design by Tanya Bäck, www.tanyabackdesigns.com

Dedicated to my Stinks, Ted,
Albie and Dusty

Preface

You may or may not have read my first book. I'm not doing a sales pitch here but it would probably be a good idea to read that first. It will explain how I got to where I am today – which is still Bolton! So technically, not very far in that sense. But it explains the shite that I have been through and also the amazing times I have had getting here.

But in brief, I'm a cop, I'm married to Adam and I have three very stinky boys: Ted and Albie, who live with us, and Dusty who lives in heaven (obviously, I can't say for sure Dusty is stinky, but as he is a boy and mine, then I'm guessing he is). I have a stinky stepson, Callum, who gives me an insight into what life will be like when the Stinks are fifteen years old. I'm thinking book three?

After believing that I had been dealt with all the trauma I was going to be dealt with, I was then diagnosed with a brain tumour. Obviously that went well, as I'm now writing my second book.

Don't get me wrong, I don't want you to feel sorry for me as I love my life, it's just a bit effin' hard sometimes, as I'm sure yours is too.

I am not writing this to tell you that I am the most amazeballs mum/ wife with everything sorted and THE PLAN for how my life should be. I am writing this to show others that we all go through bad times. When you are in that moment you think that it is the worst possible thing that can happen. I'm writing this to show you that you will be able to laugh again and life does go on, you just need to look for those effin' rainbows, no matter how faint. I aim to do this by sharing stories from my life and giving you some tools you may want to try. Not everything will work for everyone because we're all different, but equally we're all capable of amazing things we never even realised, until we tried.

I am fully aware of my failings as a parent/wife, et cetera, so to prevent anyone from reporting me to social services, I have also invited friends to share their stories too. This is for three reasons:

Reason 1: I don't look too bad as a parent/wife.

Reason 2: Reading someone else's story may resonate with you.

Reason 3: You don't get bored of my ramblings.

Writing a book is something I never thought I could achieve, so now I've achieved it, I want to keep on writing. Writing is good for the soul, and for me is like therapy without the cost. I started writing because of Dusty and it is like our thing now, so I'm not planning on stopping anytime soon.

While thinking on what I could write about next, seeing as though I covered the first forty odd years of my life in Book One (Did I tell you I've already written a book – *Look for the effin' rainbows?*), I struggled. I didn't want to go through any other major traumatic events just so I had writing material. I was in a quandary.

During my many battles in life, I paid for counselling, I had sessions with a life coach, I booked on retreats to find myself, I did a meditation course, I spoke at women's networking events – all of which I thoroughly enjoyed. But I did question where someone who couldn't afford these things go? Someone who didn't have the time or resources to get to events or courses? How would they find themselves?

Another thing that helped me was reading, mostly self-help books, but books about how real people get through life. On reading the reviews I received from Book One, I realised that I had inadvertently written a self-help book. The definition of a self-help book is *Any book which is written with the explicit intentions of helping its reader change or improves some aspects of their lives.*

OK, so Book One wasn't written with the explicit intention of helping readers to change or improve some aspect of their lives, but the comments I received showed that it did exactly that for some people – let's not split hairs.

So now I'm introducing you to my second 'self-help' book.

I have no qualifications in wellbeing, counselling or coaching. My only trophy is 'most improved player' in a women's rounders team in 2014. I shared that with a nine year old – that must count for something. What I do have is experience, and I have experienced lots of things in life and I'm very honest. As I say, I've also been on lots of courses, retreats and coaching sessions (and that wasn't for the rounders), as well as read lots of books and have used what I learned to deal with my own setbacks in life.

I'm not going to be telling you what to do in life. All I'm telling you is how I coped with life, and the tips and tools I used on the way. Life can get better.

You may read my books as you are going through similar things, and hearing someone else's story might help you – although you might also read my books and think, "Thank fuck I haven't got Irene's life!", which in turn will also help you, as you will appreciate what you do have, so it's a win-win.

Every day is a school day (little did I know how true that would be from March onwards), so after each chapter you will find a few life lessons I have learnt along the way.

Look at me as an alternative life coach, do exactly the opposite to what I do, and you'll live a long and happy life.

January

2020 started with a bang, with Adam and me going to Reykjavik for a long weekend. (Not that sort of bang – you and your filthy mind!) Adam had turned forty the previous November and Iceland was on my list of places to visit – seems fair! I'd mentioned it so much I think I'd managed to convince Adam it was a place he would love to visit too. Lesson number 1: go on about it enough and you will convince the other person it was their idea. The Stinks have learnt this art from me.

A friend recently called this a 'We Holiday', where you buy the holiday for another person but it's for the both of you. And you have full say of what you do because you are planning the trip. I think I'm going to be booking lots more 'We Holidays' as I like that arrangement.

Thankfully, our parents were happy to look after the Stinks. We had never left the Stinks before for this length of time. (I did go to London for two nights with work when Ted was two years old and he still makes comments like "Remember that time you went to London for a year." Talk about laying it on thick!)

To make things easy (ier), I had compiled a timetable for where the Stinks would be and when. (To give the appearance of a perfect daughter and mother.) Just before we left I sneaked in the fact that Barney and Flip Flop, the dog and cat, also needed looking after.

I say they happily offered but that's probably too strong a word. Either way, we went without them — the kids, not my parents — and it was amazing!

We aren't flashy people and expensive restaurants don't really float our boat – which is good, as in Iceland we couldn't afford posh grub anyway. We lived off street vendors' food and crisps. I was now in my second year of being tee total, thank God, as we couldn't have afforded wine, especially in the amounts I liked. We found an amazing coffee shop who did the most calorific cakes so we helped them out by giving them lots of our business. Still, just being there was a dream come true and the perfect start to OUR YEAR as we had christened it.

For the full tourist experience, I booked day trips for whilst we were there, our first one being the Blue Lagoon. The idea of the Blue Lagoon amazed me and I couldn't wait to get there. Iceland had been on my vision board for about ten years. I love snow (when I don't have to drive in it) and the idea of having a holiday there appealed to me as it is full of what seems like out-of-this-world features that I longed to see for myself. So there we were, on the coach with all the other day trippers, eagerly looking out of the window to catch the first glimpse of the Blue Lagoon, this ~~stunning marvel~~ tourist trap – but more on that later!

I gazed into the distance and saw steam coming up from what I thought was the ground. Beside myself with excitement, I shouted to Adam, "Wow, look at that! Isn't it amazing! We're here." All the other passengers grappled to get to my side of the coach to see what I could see, to capture their first glimpse of the phenomenon. Adam went on to explain that the steam was billowing from a factory and not, in fact, the Blue Lagoon. I felt like such a tit!

I didn't make eye contact with the rest of the day trippers after that.

Once we finally got to THE Blue Lagoon, we split up into male and female changing rooms then met outside. I was going through one of my slim'mer' stages so had purchased a bikini. This bikini was slightly different to the bikinis I wore back in the day. This one needed structure and bigger bottoms to hide my c section and (maybe a few cakes) belly, but it was a bikini all the same. I can't remember ever wearing a bikini post kids, but 2019 was a year of self-love for me after my brain surgery and I was learning to love my body (including the extra bits that I had acquired over the years). So, I went for it.

A tip my mum once told me was it's all about confidence. Confidence is attractive. If you walk into a bar with your head held high, you look great. So, I strutted my stuff in my bikini as much as I could. Once out of the changing rooms we were handed big white fluffy dressing gowns and directed to the exit doors. I had to wait for Adam — how long does it take for a bloke to get undressed? We held hands to brace ourselves for the cold. The floors were wooden and icy, not ideal for walking elegantly. There were hooks to put our new dressing gowns on. Ideally, I wanted to whip off the dressing gown, turn to Adam and see him gasp in delight, looking at me in a bikini, but in reality we both took off our dressing gowns and shuffled as quickly as we could on icy wooden floors to get into the water whilst I was breathing in as much as I possibly could without falling over. I had to cover my boobs, hiding my very erect nipples. And we all know what happens to blokes when they are cold – that's the excuse Adam was giving anyway. It felt like we were standing on top of a mountain in our underwear it was that cold. Trying to look confident had completely gone out of the window.

Being in the Blue Lagoon did feel amazing, but was not as I thought. It's very commercialised – which I understand – but we could have been at an outdoor pool at David Lloyd. I had to keep reminding myself about where I was and how many years it had been there and what an anomaly it really is.

They told us to try out the algae mask which was made of natural ingredients from the local area as we needed to experience the biotic wonders of geothermal seawater. It is supposed to increase collagen and nourish the skin from within. Apparently, it can help reduce the *appearance* of wrinkles and lines. I tried it, but realistically I need something that *removed* the wrinkles and lines, not just the appearance of them. (There was a full range of products for sale in the Blue Lagoon gift shop – no surprise there!)

But we joined in and lathered what looked like yoghurt all over our faces and swam around. Personally, I think it was just what they did for kicks. Let's get these tourists here, pretend this pool has been around for thousands of years and stick yoghurt on their faces.

The Blue Lagoon isn't in fact a natural phenomenon; it is man-made and the water is from a nearby geothermal power plant (the steam you see coming from a factory which could easily be mistaken for the Blue Lagoon – honest!) It was formed in 1976 – the same year I was formed.

After thirty minutes, I was done. I haven't got much patience. If I take the kids to the park I get bored. I need to be doing, not hanging around. Adam, however, made me stay in there longer.

Yes, I know, I really do need to slow down and appreciate my surroundings, but sometimes I treat life like a series of tick boxes, and once I've done something, move onto the next without appreciating what is around me. Hey, I'm always learning!

On the second day, Thursday, we walked around Reykjavik. I hadn't realised how small it is until we'd pretty much done it all in a couple of hours.

It was just how I had imagined. The little houses looked like the house from Hansel and Gretel, there were fairy lights everywhere — and who doesn't love fairy lights? We were wrapped up with our thermals and anything else I could wear. Adam and I looked so in love because we didn't want to leave each other's sides, but that was just for the heat source. I knew it was going to be cold but wow! If you're planning on going, buy a balaclava, forget fashion. Usually on any holiday we go on, I inevitably pack the wrong shoes and end up in the first couple of hours with feet full of blisters, but this trip I'd packed for comfort – must be my age!

During our ramblings we stopped at the cathedral. I'm not religious per se but always seem to visit churches when we are abroad; I think I'm just trying to cover all bases for when I die. (Although I'm sure I never visited a church in Kavos in 1999 on my 18's to 30's holiday, and if I did visit a church, I was pissed and I don't remember it – so it *could* be another age thing.)

The cathedral is on the top of a hill, and at over seventy metres tall, looks magnificent in its simplicity. It has a modern look to it and was all lit up. As we approached the two enormous wooden doors, we saw there was a sign to say there was a music meditation starting in five minutes. As I was now in the process of trying new things, I asked Adam if he minded if we went in. It was freezing so I think Adam would have agreed to anything just to get indoors. So, we went in and sat in silence with about five random people listening to a guy on the organ for an hour. I kept closing my eyes waiting for some divine feeling, but I never got it. But at least we were warm, and I *had* tried.

But that was a rookie mistake. As Adam had happily sat in a church listening to random organ music at my request, he then asked if I would go a record shop with him. Fuuuck! Through gritted teeth, I agreed. Two hours I spent sat on a scuffed brown leather sofa while Adam walked around and around and around a small effin' record shop.

Whilst sat there I was perusing (aka noseying/wasting time/comparing myself to others) through social media when I saw an article called 'Mothers'. It was asking mums from all over the UK to answer a series of questions about their expectations versus the reality of motherhood. Oh, I'm an expert at this. My whole life is a series of reality versus expectations and never the twain shall meet.

All I had to do was submit my answers and we would get a free photoshoot of me and the Stinks. As I had some time on my hands, I read through the questions and started to type my answers. The first question was about the expectations of motherhood compared to the reality of motherhood. Okay, how honest should I be? I decided to go for brutally honesty: "Yes, my reality of motherhood wasn't quite what I expected. I would liken it to being hit over the head with a cricket bat from out of nowhere." Next question? Has being a mum changed your attitude to work? "Yes, work is now a major inconvenience and how anyone is expected to bring up children and work full time deserves an effin' medal because it's bloody hard and full on. However, I continue to work as I need money to buy the outrageously priced Fortnite cards and all the other irrelevant bits of shite they insist they need or their lives won't be worth living." Pressed submit and thought nothing more of it.

After a looong two hours, Adam had found what he was looking for. I assumed that as we were in Iceland and that he had spent two hours looking it would be something that wasn't available in the UK, some Icelandic Indie group that was unsigned, but he walked away with a Liam Gallagher vinyl and seemed very pleased with himself. Are you kidding? I consoled myself about my wasted afternoon by popping back into the cake shop to try another of their delights.

We had – and when I saw 'we', as it was a 'we' holiday, of course I mean 'I' – also booked on a trip to see the Northern Lights. We knew that it was hit and miss if we would see them, and just because there was a coach load of sixty people attending, it didn't mean they would switch on like Blackpool illuminations but we were hopeful all the same.

We arrived at midnight and my God was it cold. We had wrapped up. Fashion has gone out of the window and I didn't care that I looked like the marshmallow man from Ghostbusters. I even bought thermal underwear for the occasion for both of us! That's what happens after you have kids. That's what I've told Adam anyway.

Once off the coach, as it had taken two hours to get there, everyone needed the toilet. Obviously, the queue for the ladies was about four times longer than the queue for the male toilets. There were only two toilets and it didn't help that everyone was wearing five layers of clothes. Once everyone was sufficiently relieved and re-dressed we went to find the best spot to stand. The tour guide advised us that the best view was from the coastal wall, so as well as the cold, we were being whipped across our faces with an almighty wind. I wasn't complaining, I was about to tick another thing off my bucket list – although Adam isn't really a fan of the cold so I could tell his patience was wearing thin.

We all stood there looking up to the sky, hoping for a glimmer of green or blue lights. It was tricky as I had to keep one eye on Adam too as it was so slippy being next to the sea. The ground was like an ice rink. Oh, don't get me wrong, it wasn't from any overly loving wife behaviour of wanting to keep my husband safe. I didn't want to miss the opportunity of recording Adam slipping on the ice, but then capturing the Northern Lights was appealing too. After an hour of looking up, our necks started to ache, our snot was frozen, people conceded defeat and slowly but surely started getting back on the coach.

Adam and I followed.

A couple of minutes later the coach driver jumped onto the coach shouting, "The Northern Lights, the Northern Lights!" Everyone scrambled to get their layers back on, pushing and shoving to get off the coach first. We saw them, and they were glorious. Not like on the postcards you see, but we did see them fleetingly and it was magical. (And by fleetingly, I mean fleetingly – we're talking ten seconds of magical lights here.)

After about forty minutes of trying to see them again and capture them on my phone (obvs for social media purposes) we again conceded and got back on the coach. Within minutes the same thing happened again – cue everyone pushing and shoving to get off the coach.

This happened a third time and everyone jumped up. Are you effin' kidding me? I turned to Adam and said, "Sack this, we could be doing this all night. We've seen them, I've ticked that box, let's just stay warm." So Adam and I stayed on the coach like miserable gets, snuggled up together whilst everyone else got freezing cold again.

All in all, we had a lovely time. Sometimes we just need adult time. Don't get me wrong, I love the Stinks and love our holidays – as manic as they are – but I also love time for just me and Adam, to remember why we got married in the first place. We are rubbish at date nights. We are constantly saying we need a night out and then something else always becomes more of a priority.

When we aren't with the Stinks, we just fall into how we used to be before all the responsibilities. It was reassuring to know that when the Stinks move out eventually, me and Adam will be okay. You see, this is the kind of shite I worry about. No wonder my head is full!

KERRY'S STORY
Why it's better to go abroad without kids

When Dillon was two and Levi was five, we were in Ibiza having lunch in a restaurant. Dillon was getting tired and cranky and he started crying. I was younger/slimmer then and was wearing a skirt and a cropped top (no bra cos my boobs hadn't lost their backbones back then) and I carried him full length under my arm out of the restaurant with him paddying. Everybody turned/watched/stared, etc. When I got outside, I glanced down and his foot had lifted one side of my top. I'd walked the complete length of the restaurant thinking everyone was staring at the red-faced screaming brat, when all the time I'd done that walk with one tit out! It was before mobile phones and I had to wait outside until Nick realised I wasn't coming back in. I was too ashamed!

On our way back to the airport, I texted home just to check everything was OK. I was expecting Ted and Albie to give me a list of presents they wanted from the airport – they had no chance with the prices in Iceland. What I did get was a photo of Ted in hospital with a cannula in his arm and a message saying Ted had been poorly but was home now!

The panic. The guilt. That's it, I was never leaving them again. This was karma getting us back for thinking we could have a sneaky trip away without them.

My mum had collected Ted from school on the Friday and he had not seemed his usual chaotic self. He had decided to go to bed early, which is unheard of at his Nan's as they have movies, a dirty stop-up night, popcorn and treats, and all share the same bed. None of which he is allowed at home. Ted went to bed and woke the next morning with a raging temperature and aching bones. He couldn't get out of bed. My mum took the decision to go to Accident and Emergency where they kept him in. He had numerous tests whilst there and was sent home with a diagnosis of a virus (otherwise known as 'the doctors had no idea'). Looking back now, I think I may have an idea of what it was!

On the plane journey home, we couldn't land for forty-five minutes due to fog, so we were just circling around the airport. I nearly broke into the cockpit myself saying, "My baby has a temperature and he needs cuddles, I'll land the effin' plane myself!" But wasn't sure if that would be a tad dramatic. I did text two friends with whom I had tentatively booked girly weekends away, stating that I was now cancelling all plans till the Stinks were married with their own Stinks. I must remember to be less hasty.

Thankfully, by the time we got home he was on the mend, but it didn't stop the guilt. The guilt lasted about a week, but after normality had resumed and the guilt had faded, I was back to looking for more sneaky trips away for Adam and I, plus I had to text my friends again about rearranging our girly weekends. 2020 was going to be a year of sneaky trips away to Amsterdam, London and maybe even fit in a week in the sun somewhere.

THE THINGS I AM GRATEFUL FOR IN 2020:

• Our trip to Iceland on our own.

• Knowing me and Adam were going to grow old together and have something to talk about.

• Thermals.

SELF-HELP TOOL

Taking time out for us.

It is important to take time out. Life gets so busy, especially in a manic household like ours, but it is essential to stay sane(ish). It should be part of your self-care. It doesn't have to be a weekend or even a night away, just a couple of hours when the kids are at school to go for lunch for a few hours and pretend you have no responsibilities. It will all still be there waiting for you when you get home, but you will be in a better frame of mind to tackle it and everyone in the family benefits in the long run.

Build a life
THAT YOU DON'T NEED
A VACATION FROM...
OR MAKE SHIT LOADS
OF MONEY SO YOU
CAN GO ANYWHERE
YOU WANT.

February

Once home from our trip, I'd had a reply from my 'Mothers' article – remember, the one I filled in while waiting for Adam in the record shop – and the photographer wanted to come over to capture the delights of our family the following week. I was excited because I had been worried I had maybe been too honest with my answers. The Stinks were excited too, that some stranger was coming to our house to take their photographs. I planned mine and the Stinks' outfits in great detail. We had to look like we hadn't over tried, so we could say, "What, these old things?" but really, I'd spent a fortune on my Next directory, coordinating our outfits for the day of the photoshoot (without Adam's knowledge of what I'd spent but I'm guessing this probably goes without saying). We all had an element of blue in our outfits – matching without over matching is key.

Just before the photographer (a lovely lady called Rebecca) arrived, I got the vacuum out to do one last swoop of the room. In my haste, I vacuumed up the blind in the lounge. (I know, how is that even possible?) As I panicked, I yanked at the vacuum and pulled down the blind fitting from the ceiling. Great!

"Muuuum," I heard Albie shout from the top of the stairs, "I've wiped my bum myself," and with that I heard thump, thump, thump. That was Albie coming downstairs on his bare arse so I could check his bum!

It was like slow motion – me running to the stairs to stop every step being covered in skids, but as I still had the vacuum in my hand (which was still attached to the blind), I was just too slow. Albie had reached the bottom step. "Teeeedddd," I screamed, "get the baby wipes out quick." He had managed to leave a skid on every single step. That takes skill that does.

The house was spotless, minus one blind and plus a couple of tiny skids by the time I'd used up half a pack of baby wipes. I was a hot, sweaty mess. The photographer wanted natural shots of us, as though she wasn't in the room. But really, if she hadn't been in the room, I would have been screaming like a banshee and the Stinks would have been fighting.

She was asking me questions about the answers I had submitted while casually taking shots. "So when you say you would liken motherhood to being hit around the head with a cricket bat, what did you mean?" "Erm, I meant it was like someone had hit me around the head with a cricket bat..." "Oh," Rebecca replied politely.

In all honesty, Ted and Albie acted like animals. It started to get a bit raucous when the photographer said, "Why don't you both jump off the sofa and I will try to get you mid-air." That was all the encouragement they needed. They were naturals. Naturals if you were photographing the monkeys at Knowsley Safari park!

I've no idea how I didn't bollock them while she was there. A short time later, she had enough images and was leaving. I think she couldn't get out of the house quick enough personally. I was waving at the door whilst Ted was hanging from around my neck and Albie hanging from Ted's neck.

As soon as the door closed, I flicked them off my back and turned to look at them with a face like thunder. "Get your arses upstairs now!"

The photos turned out great and the Stinks actually look like pleasant children. You would never have known. The art of still images.

As 2020 was the year that I was going to release my first book to the world, I needed to do more blogs and get myself out there as an author. Even saying that now seems a bit weird. I say it like how your grandma may say certain words, you know the words I mean. Like it's a dirty word, like 'time of the month'. But I needed to own this and, like I said before, it's all about the confidence. My book had been edited and re-edited and was ready to go. I had been writing it for what felt like years and I think I used it as a bit of a comfort blanket. When people asked about my book, my answer was always, "Oh, I'm still writing it, it will be ready soon." I think I was perhaps stalling because it just seemed too scary to get the book out there.

I have to put a date on any of my goals because if I didn't I would put them off forever and that date was now.

The definition of an author is *a person who writes a book, article or document* so I was one, I just needed to believe it.

I thought I had done the hard part by writing it, but it was only now when it was ready to go on sale that I discovered that I had to market it. How the bloody hell do I go about that? I often feel like I'm just winging it at everything in life, but isn't everyone?

So now, between looking after the Stinks, cleaning (I use that term loosely), and working full time, I now had to become an expert at marketing. I did a few blogs for different businesses and signed up on Twitter and LinkedIn. Twitter, I still can't get my head around. LinkedIn is more formal and serious. But that's just not me. I stuck with Instagram and Facebook, or as my mother-in-law would say, 'The Facebook'. I read books on marketing and joined courses on how to get the best out of your social media. After all my research, I decided, 'I know what I *can* do, I can have a launch party.' If Carrie Bradshaw could have one, then so could I! Listing that as one my goals for April, what could possibly go wrong there?

I tried to get a literary agent as I thought that was what I needed. You don't just pick one though, you need to research them and see if they would be right for you, and you for them. After hours of researching, I spent two hours one evening compiling my submission to my chosen agent. In my covering letter, I tried to be funny yet professional – I struggle with the professional part. It took forever. Finally, after checking and rechecking, I sent my submission and waited.

I looked at my emails probably about a hundred times in the next hour, but nothing. I expected an email saying they had received it.

The next morning, still no email, so I went over my submission. I'd only gone and written the wrong effin' email address. A mixture between my own email address and my work's email address. Fuuuck! This is me all over. I rang the agent and left a message. I never heard from them.

Adam was doing his thing too. His hobby and passion is music. So last year I bought him a mixer, or something like that that you play music on. I don't really know what I bought him, but he liked it. He had started DJing, not at 21st parties and Bar mitzvahs, but in venues in Manchester, pre-show parties and aftershow parties for the likes of Noel Gallagher and Richard Ashcroft. He was acing it. His twitter account had over eight thousand followers and he had got bookings for Kendal Calling and Shine On. (I wouldn't know what these were if it wasn't for Adam, but for people like me, these are festivals.) Playing at festivals was a dream come true (apart from marrying me) for Adam. 2020 was going to be Adam's year too!

Adam isn't like me, he doesn't spend months procrastinating and thinking of reasons why he shouldn't do it. He just does it. I admire him for that.

He arranged a pre-show and aftershow for the Liam Gallagher gig in Amsterdam. Go big or go home I suppose! That's great, Adam, but you're not going to Amsterdam on your own…no way!

The closer it got, the more anxious I felt about it, as I still hadn't sorted out childcare. And because of the last time, I thought our parents would think we were taking the piss. I was also a bit cautious, because since staying with my mum, Ted had once shouted out "That man ain't got no dick" in an American accent. I was shocked. "Oh my God! Where have you heard that, Ted?" "From Nan." I couldn't believe it. I thought maybe it was a ploy to not have them for a long weekend again. A couple of hours later, Ted said, "Oh sorry, it was from Ghostbusters!" How on earth you get Nan and a Ghostbuster mixed up, I'll never know.

Before I even thought of asking either set of parents for another pass, Adam and I chatted about what music he would be playing and the fact that I didn't know hardly any of it! I would have to make up my own words to look like I was joining in. I asked what time the aftershow started. 11pm. Wow! Since my brain surgery, I never go to bed later than 9pm. Plus, I was now eighteen months into my decision to go sober. The thought of making up my own words, trying to sober dance and be out past my bedtime wasn't very appealing, so I opted out.

I think Adam was secretly pleased. Surely he was going to make it up to me for Valentine's Day and my birthday, which were both in the same month as Amsterdam.

It was my 44th birthday. Now I know I'm probably in the minority here, but I expect the same effort now as I got for my ninth birthday. I'm more into memories and experiences now as opposed to tangible gifts. That doesn't necessarily mean a large amount of money spent on me (although I wouldn't complain), but definitely some effort has to be made.

I like to put lots of effort into people's birthday, try to think outside the box. Sometimes I fail. As you know by now, I'm all about finding myself and thought I'd buy my sister Catherine (the crazy one) a session with a life coach. I think the life coach may have retired after her session with Catherine. When my sister spoke to me afterwards she said, "Thanks for the present but never ever buy me anything like that again." But at least I try. It's like the card you receive. The card is very important. I always read the words in a card. I can't buy a batch and just pull one out of the cupboard. Although, that would be a lot easier and less hassle. One year, I bought one for my dad, a Father's Day card saying, 'To My Husband on Father's Day' in big letters, which I didn't notice before posting. Didn't read that one, did I?

Any person's birthday in our house is an event. They have breakfast in bed, banners, balloons (although I hate balloons, so the day after I go around and pop them all), party poppers and, most importantly, cake. You keep your birthday cards up for one week. As I'm writing this, I know I'm sounding a bit like a 'you can have fun, as long as it's organised fun' kinda person, but it seems to work in our house.

ZOE'S STORY
I want to be alone

On Ruby's 4th birthday party, we had gone all out. We hired an entertainer, a pirate and a mermaid and had thirty of her friends there.

Ruby spent the whole party sat under a table and didn't join in a single game or activity.

Once home she proceeded to tell us it was the best birthday party she had ever had.

Adam and I have been together twelve years and he knows how much weight I place on my birthday…but he's getting shitter and shitter as the years go on. He is not arsed about his birthday, which is fine, but he still gets the banners and balloons, whether he wants them or not! I'm sure deep down he loves it.

A few years ago, I had to ask him if I could have breakfast in bed on my birthday, to which he replied, "Do you have sugar in your coffee?" FUMING! I have never, ever drunk coffee.

I do like surprises, but then again I pride myself on my detective skills (on that note, don't ever play Cluedo with me) and finding out what I am getting, so I understand why people don't bother with surprises for me anymore. It must get a tad tedious me ruining them all.

Case in point: years ago, when I knew Adam had enquired about buying my engagement ring, I was getting frustrated waiting around. I asked him if had he got the ring and he told me it was being shipped over from their shop in Brussels. So I researched it. No shop in Brussels. Ha, I knew it! He'd got it. So I booked myself in for a manicure, waited and practised my surprised face. My surprised face was impressive and it wasn't until Adam read my first book that he realised I knew the proposal was imminent.

When I get a gift that isn't quite me, I try to hide it, but my face gives it away big time. To be fair, sometimes people don't make it easy. One Christmas, Adam and I had a £50 limit as we were saving for a new house – and he bought me a box of fireworks…A BOX OF FIREWORKS! I do love fireworks at Disney World or on November 5th, but not for a present – and my only present at that. I couldn't hide my disappointment that day. We were in bed, pre-kids, as I unwrapped this intriguing box in excitement. I just placed my fireworks at the side of the bed and went back to sleep. He's still convinced this was a good gift.

Another birthday, he organised for us to go on a weekend away, which was a lovely gift. We had a glorious time away the weekend before my birthday. However, I still wanted full effort on my birthday, which was on the following Sunday. But instead, on the Friday he said, "There are some flowers in the kitchen for you," and went into the lounge to switch on the TV. I followed him, saying, "Oh right, that's nice of you to get me some flowers for no reason as I assume they are not for my birthday as my birthday isn't till Sunday?" He thought I was acting like a child.

…maybe I was, but I don't care (said as I throw myself on the floor, rolling around, kicking and screaming!)

(NB: Adam did excel with my present this year – a framed copy of my very first book! I loved it!)

If you are man reading this, then here are a few tips of what to get your significant other:
- A spa day – with that you need to organise child care.
- Jewellery – can be a bit tricky, but consult significant others sisters, mums or best friends.
- A thoughtful gift – photo of the kids framed, ideally with their mum in the photo.
- Buy their wish list on Amazon – or some of it.

- Underwear – this is a tricky one. If you are newly together, buy sexy underwear but not slutty, there's a difference (Google it). If you have been together a while, maybe a voucher to a lingerie shop. (M& S is not a lingerie shop)
- Take her out for a meal but don't just book a table. Again, you need to organise the child care, taxis, everything that goes with it, and book her a hairdresser's appointment for the day of meal.

THE THINGS I AM GRATEFUL FOR IN 2020:

• Becoming an author.

• The art of still images.

• On the odd occasion, Adam can still get me thoughtful gifts.

GIFTS THAT MY FRIENDS RECEIVED FROM THEIR OTHER HALVES

WHICH DIDN'T QUITE HIT THE SPOT

WILL YOUNG CD FOR TWO
CONSECUTIVE VALENTINE'S DAYS

ODD SHOES

HAIRBRUSH

HAIR GEL FOR A BALD MAN

DRAWER LINERS

DECORATIVE HEEL CLIPS (I MEAN, WHAT THE..?)

SELF-HELP TOOL
Goal Setting

Write your goals down and put a date for when you want to achieve them. Put some easy ones on the list but put some on the list that scare you even reading them. These are the ones you are going to smash.

Here were my goals for 2020:

- Being happy at work with no stress and hours that suit me – tick (see March)
- Pay off credit card – tick (I paid off that specific credit card by doing a balance transfer to another card.)
- Lose 31lb by December – As I'm writing this it is 18th December. I have lost 3lb so 28lb in thirteen days is doable, right?
- Stay alcohol free – tick (Very proud of myself on that one.)
- Having a book published – tick (Did I tell you I've writt...?)
- Having a book launch – nope
- Having a photo in a bikini and not being scared to share it on social media – tick (Although it was just my top half. Bottom half is on next year's goal list.)
- 10k run – nope (Still on week three of couch to 5K.)

Looking back, I didn't do too badly. But that's another thing you must do, always look back and see what you have achieved and celebrate those achievements.

If you were able to

believe

IN FATHER CHRISTMAS FOR EIGHT YEARS, YOU CAN BELIEVE IN YOURSELF FOR FIVE MINUTES.

March

As I've already said, I had decided that 2020 was going to my year – especially after everything that had happened the year before. I had dealt with Brian the brain tumour and I was coming back fighting. I had finished writing my book (in Dusty's name) and published it. Me, Irene Wignall, who can't spell for tofee (Do you like what I did there?), had written a book that was out there for anyone to read. Due to the lack of publishing companies banging on my door, I decided to self-publish. Sounds easy. All you need to do is upload it on Amazon and they do the rest. Oh my God, the amount of stress that caused me was insane! Why are things never easy? I assumed – again wrongly – that once it was out there everyone would be clamouring to buy it.

It felt amazing, exhilarating, incredible, scary, and unnerving. (Can you tell I used a thesaurus here?) I felt like an imposter and vulnerable all at the same time. What if it was shite? Who did I think I was? I mean, really? Why couldn't I just be happy with my lot and leave it at that?

I'm sure we all get that feeling from time to time and I'd love to say I rose above it, but in all reality, I still feel like that now. And I'm doing it all again!

But I was going to ignore that niggling thought and go for it anyway. I was getting my shit together. I was meditating. I had still given up on the alcohol. The Stinks were happy. Adam and I had managed to escape for a couple of days. I was getting a new car. Things were looking bright. This was going to be a great year.

Let's do this…cue…

An effin' LOCKDOWN!!!!

Wow, who could have predicted that one?

As Adam and I are keyworkers, the Stinks could have continued going to school, but we sat and chatted through it and decided that we didn't want the Stinks taking any unnecessary risks if we could help it. We would keep them at home and home-school them, working at home some days and working our shifts around them. We have handled worse times; we had this one under the belt.

Can I just point out here that this was when we thought lockdown was going to be three weeks long, not three effin' months!

I'm a big believer in affirmations – although I have learnt along the way I need to be quite specific. One of my affirmations for a long time was to spend more quality time with the Stinks. I have wished for this for a few years now. I kept thinking that if I could just get a couple of months off work with the Stinks while they were little, I would be happy. Then I got Brian the brain tumour – not the kind of time off work I was thinking – so I got more specific with my affirmations. If I could have just a couple months off with the Stinks and no one was ill – so we get a lockdown! Hey ho! I'll try a different approach next year.

Having said that, I started out in all good faith. This was going to work. We were going to be a team, a perfect picture of family unity. I printed off pictures and worksheets for us to make our own time capsule. I bought face paints. The Amazon delivery guy was risking his life daily delivering *essential* items to our house.

School printed off worksheets. I subscribed to every educational app going, most free for the first month. ("Must remember to cancel after the first month," she says eight months later.)

It wasn't only the Stinks who were going to get educated. I decided I was going to use this time wisely. I enrolled on lots of courses – Marketing, Wellbeing, you name it, my name was on the list.

I say we were in lockdown like it's a common thing. I'd probably never said the word before this year and now I said it in every sentence.

Working from home is something I've always wanted to do. Waking up at a reasonable hour, not having to put makeup on, hair tied up, pj's on, able to put a load of washing on throughout the day… Perfect, or so I thought.

Initially I thought it would be fun to look at the Stinks as my co-workers. Because the Stinks *would* be my co-workers for the foreseeable, I would be seeing them daily, moaning to them about their dad, telling them how much my kids were doing my head in, the usual stuff you chat about with your co-workers.

We could work together as a team – how wrong was I!

I am naturally a very organised person, I had this completely under control. A breeze, I thought.

Day one of home-schooling went a bit like this:

I subscribe to Joe Wicks PE Lesson and I sit and write a timetable. I give my co-workers one pound in change so they can buy snacks throughout the day, teaching them the value of money. Maybe I should partake in this lesson too? I obviously share all this on social media just to prove how much I am acing this home-schooling lark.

They run out of money before lunch. We attempt Joe Wicks. My co-workers, for about thirty seconds, then sit and watch me complete the rest. I was a hot sweaty mess by the end of it. I had to re-check this was aimed at getting kids active. Jesus, I worked harder that morning than my body combat classes at the gym.

I set out our office/classroom on the dining room table, give them some tasks, then prepare to open my emails.

Having addressed one email, I then hear, "Mummy, how do I do this?" "Mummy, where is the iPad?" "Mummy, my co-worker has just punched me."

Right, let's break for lunch. And fifteen minutes of whatever you want to do. iPad out, their fifteen minutes turn into an hour while I address emails two, three and four.

I master the art of feigning interest whilst being talked at simultaneously about Roblox and Minecraft.

We paint each other's faces – Art lesson completed.

Guilt sets in. They need fresh air. Right, go on the trampoline and jump one hundred times each, whilst counting – Maths lesson completed.

Whilst my co-workers are jumping and counting, emails five and six are addressed.

Give my co-workers two Lego sets to complete; they can improve their fine motor skills and problem solving. We haven't had Lego in our house before. I didn't know that I have to find each tiny piece for them! No emails addressed.

Mid-afternoon, my co-workers have a fight. I walk away and put myself in a dark room for thirty minutes. I try some meditation. Again, guilt sets in. I come down to find my co-workers have barricaded the lounge door to stop me from coming back in. The little shites!

That evening, whilst feeling worn out and defeated yet relieved we had survived day one of home-schooling, I took Albie to bed. Walking up the stairs, we found a small piece of Lego. I joked and said, "Look Albie, it's a piece of your nose!" He laughed then he took the piece and said the same to me so I learned forward and closed my eyes…and he shoved the piece up my nose. Jesus Christ, Albie, I didn't expect that! I struggled to get the piece out and thought, 'Shit, the NHS are stretched enough at the moment, there's no way I can go to Accident and Emergency with a piece of Lego up my left nostril.' Thankfully, with a bit of struggle and some vegetable oil, I retrieved it.

Note to self: don't close your eyes around Albie.

As part of the wellbeing team at work, I offered to do a blog about how well I was doing with the whole working from home /home-schooling aspect of lockdown. I think basically people read it and thought, 'Jesus, I'm not doing that bad after all.'

I titled it 'A day in the life of a Detective/Mum/Techer/Wife and anything else you can think of'.

Yes, you read it right, I spelt the word 'teacher' wrong and didn't notice until it had been emailed to one thousand police officers. Of course I couldn't be a teacher; I couldn't even spell the effin' word!

CAROL'S STORY
How can I possibly home-school my kids?

I'm really trying, but I have one who moves from horizontal in her bed to horizontal on the floor, another one who thinks beef burgers are good for you because they don't come from cows, they come from mincemeat. And a five-year-old who constantly wants to check if I can still make milk from my boobies.

After the first couple of days, the maths lessons were getting a tad boring – counting from one to one hundred can become tedious. I ordered two of those massive balloon things that you blow up and bounce on the trampoline to keep the Stinks outside for longer. Three weeks later, I received a parcel with two baby vests in it. Are you kidding? It's an effin' scam! I sent them a very professional email with the words "This is a scam!!!" Obviously put a lot of effort and time into complaining there, Irene.

A day later I got a reply from Johnny saying in broken English, "We apologise, your goods with be with you soon." Yeah, OK Johnny.

Two days later, the balloons arrived. Oops! I knew my Amazon ordering was getting slightly out of hand but had I now resorted to buying baby vests in my sleep?

Each day we would do our daily exercise, our one walk which incorporated sweet shopping (essentials) and visiting the post office to post back all the dresses that I kept ordering from ASOS, and back home again.

One eventful day we had Barney the dog with us. Barney is my 'get better soon' dog, after my brain operation. I told Adam if he agreed to get a dog it would aid with my recovery. Barney is a white fluffy cavachon with a penchant for black cats and little man syndrome. If he sees big burly dogs he goes crazy and shies away from the small dogs. He is generally a good dog but likes to do a runner every so often, just to keep us on our toes, as he did this particular day.

The queue for the post office was about ten deep, so I told the Stinks to wait around the corner with Barney so as not to panic anyone by coughing within two metres of them. Just as I was at the front of the queue, Barney flew around the corner, no lead, and ran straight into the main road, stopping all the traffic. The Stinks were running behind him, crying and screaming.

I spent a good ten minutes running around the street like a lunatic. People standing in front of Barney trying to stop him without touching him (as no one knew then if dogs carried Covid). Eventually, I grabbed him and a random woman kindly advised me that maybe I should keep some dog treats in my pocket. Yes, thanks for that. What I actually needed was a bottle of vodka in my pocket!

The Stinks' respective teachers rang up once a week to keep in touch with them and to try to get them to do some work. I would have them on loudspeaker and the Stinks tended to just nod in answer to any questions. That would be until the teachers asked what work they had done that day. Then the Stinks proceeded to list a plethora of YouTubers they had been watching that morning. Horrified, I would be in the background laughing nervously saying, "What about that writing you did? Had you forgot about that, silly boys?"

After a couple of weeks, we lowered our expectations on home-schooling considerably. I often thought teaching was the route I should have gone down, but I know now that is isn't. I don't think you can say to pupils in your class, after they've answered a question, "Are you effin' serious!!! Is that your answer???" before walking off muttering the words, "Do it on your own now, I've had enough."

KATE'S STORY
Working from home

I set my twelve-year-old the task of washing my car on our driveway as she was having to self-isolate for two weeks due to an outbreak at school.

I was typing away when I heard her yelling for me.

Running outside, I discovered she'd managed to lean on the handbrake and my car had rolled into the garage (just missing the dog I've borrowed as ours had a heart attack when I was working from home the other week, and my husband's new motorbike - the one he forgot to tell me about, the one that arrived when I was working from home).

The office suddenly seems like a calm, appealing place to work!

My mum and Adam's mum did a couple of doorstep visits. It was heart-breaking when the Stinks saw them. I know all grandparents wanted to do was cuddle their grandchildren. I'd like to say the feelings were mutual, and I'm sure deep down they do want to cuddle Granny and Nan, but only in secret.

When I realised the lockdown wasn't going to just be three weeks as we originally thought, my motivation waivered. By now I was working from home permanently. I realised that all the courses I had enrolled on were not going to happen because I was still actually working alongside looking after the Stinks. I had no idea where I thought I was going to find time to learn more.

I couldn't be arsed to do anything, so I thought after six weeks I best make a start on something productive – and it was either exercise or this book…and this won!

I had done all the usual things, like binge-watch Tiger King, attempted baking cupcakes, and had my head in the fridge door for the majority of the time. The thing is, I shouldn't have been bored as I was still working, but if everyone else was getting fat because of Covid, I was not going to give up this chance for my eating and plumpness to be validated. I finally had a reason to be chubby.

After six weeks of eating rubbish, my skin wouldn't stretch anymore so I knew I needed to get a grip. I joined up for a thirty-day shred with a bunch of eager beavers…too eager for my liking. For those of you that haven't had the pleasure, a shred workout is high intensity workouts done for thirty days in a row to help you lose weight. What was I thinking? Joe Wicks nearly finished me off!

After taking the obligatory fat photos of myself half naked and recording all my measurements, I sent them via email to a stranger and gave him £40 for the privilege of looking at them. (That reminds me, I must check that website was legit.)

My fat photos were bad, but to be fair, I've had worse fat photos. Anyway, you never stand up straight for the 'before' photo and you have to have the obligatory sad face – it's the kind of face you pull if you find a worm in your burger and you are on the front page of the local newspaper. I bet I could look a size smaller if I just stood up straight and smiled and maybe did a bit a contouring on my body with fake tan, but I will do all that for the 'after' photos.

I was added to a group chat with strangers, and after three days I hated them all. That's a bit strong. I didn't hate them, I was just jealous of their motivation. I had stuck to the diet but we got a new exercise video every couple of days. The first one arrived on a Saturday morning. I woke up at 8am, put on my gym gear, went straight downstairs, pressed play and did five press-ups. Fuck that!!!! So I thought I best do something productive now I was up. I enjoy Zumba so I found one on YouTube, pressed play and did the thirty seconds warm up. You can do one too, Flaviola! Far too much hip thrusting and jiggling! So I sat down and scrolled though social media. Finally, something I'm good at.

I kept getting photos of the other participants' lunches in the group chat and comments like "Look at this beast of an omelette." Sorry, beast and omelette don't fit in the same sentence for me. I know I'm just jealous and I did write earlier about accepting myself and my body.

We now talk about lockdown weight like pregnancy weight, as though it's a justification as it's only your lockdown weight. So it's not like your real weight.

Once I've lost weight (again) I will feel better in myself. I will go back to the gym once they're open, but now I know working out in my own home is not my thing and I need some trim instructor bollocking me to make me do anything. I wouldn't dream of doing the walk of shame out of an exercise class at the gym. In my house, I can do the walk of shame no problem. I left the Whatsapp group. No shame felt!

We have been in this house for 9 years and I have moaned about getting garden furniture every summer. With the lockdown and our holidays being cancelled, I knew this was the time we needed it more than ever. I had a vision of the perfect family summer in the garden…exquisite meals just thrown together and presented on beautiful large plates, flickering lanterns and cashmere throws. The scents of luxurious flowers surrounding us – wasn't too much to ask for! I had to play hard ball with Adam. So a sex ban was mentioned in passing. Strangely enough, I got my furniture pretty quickly. Hmmm, now what else do I need?

Before the furniture came, Adam wanted to paint the fences and as fence paint had become another valued commodity (along with toilet roll), he was delighted when he had found some in the shed.

It can take Adam a while when it comes to things like this, but this was something he could do, albeit slowly. I offered to help, but he asked for Ted and Albie rather than me. I don't blame him, as in our old house, I bought an all-singing, all-dancing paint spray gun and then realised I had sprayed all next door's new white UPVC door in Red Cedar. So I'll give him that one this time.

Operation garden was now complete ready for our outdoorsy life.

THINGS THAT I AM GRATEFUL FOR IN 2020;

- Teachers.

- Teachers.

- Stretchy clothes.

SELF-HELP TIP

Be specific with your Affirmations. Be careful what you wish for

Affirmations are positive statements that can help you overcome self sabotaging, negative thoughts. It may sound a bit woo woo, but just try it. Start by writing down three affirmations and sticking them somewhere where you look daily, like your bathroom mirror. You need to write them as you have already achieved your goals.

Here are my three affirmations for 2020:

- I am happy we live in our forever home and we are all settled and content.
- I am happy we have no debt.
- I am happy that my book(s) are a success and now a TV show.

Obviously, mine are a work in progress. You write them down each day and really believe they are true. What's the harm in trying?

If you SEE

My Kids

LOCKED OUTSIDE TODAY,
MIND YOUR OWN
BUSINESS. WE ARE HAVING
A FIRE DRILL.

April

Now we had all the garden furniture, plus hundreds of outdoor cushions, bunting, candles, fairy lights, cashmere throws and a log burner (as you can't get the furniture without all the rest), we could at least enjoy the outdoor life. You see, the outdoor life was on my vision board. An idyllic photo of a family sat around a table enjoying food and drinks, laughing together.

On my vision board I also had a photo of my forever home. I'd seen it for sale near the Stinks' school and it was perfect, so I parked on the driveway of the house as though I was pulling up from a day at work, got out and took a photo of my car on the drive and quickly got back in the car and reversed off before I was arrested for attempted burglary.

Adam came home to photos of my car on the drive of this house tacked up in every room in the house. He assumes this is normal behaviour now and has accepted it. Well it is normal behaviour for me. The house has now sold, but that hasn't put me off. It will be ours eventually, I know it.

In a morning now, with my new furniture, I would put all the cushions out, switch on the fairy lights, arrange the throws and have a brew, bring them all back in again in case it rained, then at lunch, run back out with all the cushions, etc. sit outside having our meal for thirty minutes, then back inside with them, and do it all again in the evening.

My garden cushions were going out more than I was.

My aim was to get up before the Stinks woke. I would have my first brew of the day outside listening to the birds and perhaps throw in a quick mediation if I remembered. Only we have squeaky stairs, so as soon as I stepped on them, Albie's eyes would ping open.

I did lock them inside the house one day when they were particularly boisterous at 7am. It was bliss. I could still see them through the patio doors, kicking ten colours out of each other, so they were not neglected (as such), but I closed my eyes and turned up the volume on my meditation and enjoyed my five minutes of peace.

MARK'S STORY

Teaching children valuable lessons

I was a community beat officer. Going back to the days when police officers used to go into schools and run classes with the teachers about stranger danger. Those were the days, when everyone knew a stranger used to drive a Hillman Avenger estate and carried sweets in the glove compartment...oh how naive we were then!

Anyway, on this occasion, myself and 'Bill', my partner PC, were off to give that talk to a group of primary school children. We had worked out a new delivery method for our session and decided that one of us would be 'the stranger' and one of us would be the nice policeman. We'd act out a scenario with the children and get them to think about what they should do given a set of circumstances.

You see, today no one would let this play out, health and safety would be all over it...but this was 1987.

So we needed props. Bill would sport a 'civvy jacket' (civilian jacket) and I would be the friendly face of the local policeman.

The plan was hatched. I went in to the class, talked to all the children, made friends, showed them my truncheon (I repeat, it was 1986), handcuffs etc. On the given word "now", Bill would walk in dressed in his special outfit of civvy attire. He took his clip-on tie off too, just to make sure no one knew he was a cop 'undercover'.

"Hello everyone," Bill said whilst I was in mid flow, winning over the children's confidence about not going with someone you didn't know. "Can anyone tell me where the staff room is, or better still, could someone show me please?"

I have to say that all the children stopped, looked around at Bill and then back at me, as if to say "Oooooo, stranger."

However, there was one child (and I guess there always is) who stood up, took Bill's outstretched hand and said, "I'll show you." Off they walked, hand in hand, stranger and school kid. Our cunning plan had worked.

Bill was now outside the classroom with a teacher, talking about not going with strangers and making sure that this wouldn't happen again.

Ah, but my job wasn't over yet. My job was to carry on, ignore what had just happened in the hope that a pupil would say something.

None of the pupils said a word.

Back to plan B.

I stopped talking and looked hard at the children. "Does anyone know who that person was who just walked in?" I asked.

Silence. Some very apprehensive faces were now looking up at me as if to say "Oh oh."

"Do we think that person was a stranger?"

"STRANGER, STRANGER, STRANGER!!!" was the resounding shout from all the kids as the realisation of what had just happened sunk in.

"Why didn't you shout and stop John (the school boy who had walked out with Bill) going with a stranger?" I asked.

And it was then that a hand rose slowly from the back of the class. I was in no doubt to offer some condolence for John's departure and potential demise with a bag of sweets in Bill's Avenger.

"Yes David, why didn't you say something or shout?"

"PC Freel," came the reply, "we don't like John."

Out of the mouths of babes. Safe to say that we never employed that stranger danger role play again.

As lockdown was a bit longer than first anticipated, we needed to accept the new norm (a phrase I have grown to dislike immensely).

OTHER PHRASES AND WORDS WHICH I HAD USED VERY RARELY BEFORE THIS YEAR BUT NOW DISLIKE INTENSELY:

UNPRECEDENTED TIMES

LOCKDOWN

TIER THREE

WHERE IS YOUR MASK?

HOW MUCH TOILET PAPER HAVE WE GOT LEFT?

YOU'RE ON MUTE

YOU'RE ON MUTE AGAIN

I CAN HEAR YOU BUT I CAN'T SEE YOU

SOCIAL DISTANCING

ESSENTIAL WORKERS

KEYWORKERS

ELBOW BUMPS

DISTANCE LEARNING

YOUR BUBBLE

SELF-ISOLATING

YOUR DELIVERY IS ON ITS WAY (TEN EMAILS A DAY)

A STITCH IN TIME SAVES NINE

STAY SAFE

STAY AT HOME

STAY ALERT

PROTECT THE NHS

RULE OF SIX

HANDS, FACE, SPACE

HANDS, FACE, SPACE, VENTILATE (ADAPTED FOR THE WINTER VERSION)

EAT OUT TO HELP OUT (THAT ONE WORKED OUT WELL, DIDN'T IT!)

SHUT UP KIDS, I'M LISTENING TO BORIS

IN THIS TOGETHER

TO BE ABSOLUTELY CLEAR

WORKING TIRELESSLY

WE WILL BEAT THIS

ALAS!

We all saw the video clips of Italian people singing from their balconies, embracing the changes. However, this didn't happen in Bolton! But in the middle of all the negativity, there was plenty of evidence of humanity around (well, apart from in the toilet roll aisle in Asda). I remember reading about Janice from Nob End (yes, there really is a place in Bolton called that) who did a sponsored pasty eating challenge and raised a massive £7.85 for the NHS. She wasn't quite up there with Captain Tom but did her bit all the same.

Each Thursday I would stand outside with the Stinks clapping and banging pans. It was the only exciting thing that was happening. Albie asked where the doctors were that we were clapping for, as he looked curiously up and down the road.

Adam went to collect some food my mum had made for us one evening and just as he was leaving their garden at 8pm on a Thursday, all the neighbours clapped as he got into his car. This was the only standing ovation Adam is going to get any time soon.

We were now eating more of our meals outside – as I had hoped – although I wasn't aware there was food protocol, of which Adam informed me, thankfully.

Adam thinks you can only eat certain foods outdoors.

ALLOWED AND DISALLOWED FOODS TO EAT OUTSIDE AS PER ADAM'S RULES

ALLOWED 😎	DISALLOWED 😫
Burgers on barms (a whole different topic on barms, baps or muffins)	Curry and rice
Sandwiches	Soup
Crisps and nuts	Any dessert – although this does not include hand-held ice cream like Cornettos as they are allowed.
Sausages	Bacon
Homemade kebabs	Takeaway kebabs
Lunch and dinner allowed	Breakfast a big no no
Beer, wine, pop	Cup of tea

Even when I had managed to navigate Adam's rules on outdoor eating, each time we set everything out and cooked the appropriate food, the Stinks would spend the whole time moaning it was either too cold or then too hot. We were incredibly lucky with the weather; it was glorious and hardly any rain. Can you imagine doing a lockdown in winter? Thank God we didn't have to do that?! (Ahem!)

I want a bloody outdoorsy family so you *will* sit out and breathe in the fresh air! I have a photo of Adam, Ted and Albie all playing their guitars in the garden. They looked like the bloody Partridge family. I'm not sure, but I think playing the guitar outside (especially when you can't play the guitar) is against the rules? If not, it should be.

N.B.: It has come to our attention that one of the neighbours is smoking weed due to the smell that filters through the estate. Hmmm, maybe that's what's been giving me the munchies all along and I'm not a greedy get. I actually love the smell; if I could buy a room spray of the same smell I would have it in my bedroom!*

(*This is one of those sentences that I ask myself should I write this or tell a therapist instead?)

THREE THINGS I AM GRATEFUL FOR IN 2020:

• Garden furniture and fairy lights.

• Having Adam there so I didn't commit a cardinal sin of eating a curry outdoors.

• You can lock patio doors from the outside.

EMILY'S STORY
Our daily walk

Each day when I walked Frankie to playschool, we would walk past the most glorious garden. At the edge of the garden near the footpath was an array of sweet peas.

I would tell Frankie how much I love the smell of sweet peas and that it reminded of me when I was his age. Frankie loves hearing stories about when I was little.

One day we did our normal route and I bumped into a friend I hadn't seen for a while. We stopped and chatted for what seemed like ages, but probably wasn't longer than ten minutes.

This was enough time for Frankie to pull every sweet pea flower from the garden we had always admired.

He handed me the flowers and said, "Here Mummy, you can be little again."

It made me well up but it also made me quickly run the other way and we have never walked past that garden since.

SELF-HELP TIP
Vision boards

A vision/dream/goal board is a collage of images, pictures and affirmations of your desires, designed to serve as a source of inspiration and motivation. I often do a vision board at the beginning of a year. But that doesn't mean it has to stay the same. It can evolve as the year goes on, it's your board. I mean, we evolve all the time. I'm not the same person as I was five years ago and definitely not the same person I was twenty years ago - and that's not a bad thing. (Believe you me, if you'd have seen that cropped top and sky blue flares I wore clubbing...) It's natural, and sometimes necessary to change.

You need to have an emotional connection with everything you put on there. Don't just put on words that you think look good. When you look at it, you need to get butterflies in your stomach. A bit like I did when I first met Adam. (That sentence is for Adam's benefit.)

Just because the pictures and words are up there, you don't just forget about them, you actively work for the things on there. They are a constant reminder of what you aim to achieve.

And lastly, you need to believe these visions are going to happen.

On my vision board, I have:

- holiday destinations I'd like to take the Stinks
- holiday destinations where I'd like to go without the Stinks
- quotes that I like
- my affirmations
- words that resonate with me.

Adam initially thought it was a load of rubbish but he has sneaked a couple of goals of his own on there too. Hedging his bets, I think.

It needs to be somewhere where you can look at it often. Mine sits behind my desk, so when I'm supposed to be writing this book and I start to daydream they can be daydreams with a purpose! Preferably put it somewhere where the attendees of your Zoom meeting can't see it, especially if there is something on there you don't want them to see.

Also, be careful of what is on there if you have young, prying eyes in the house. I have a tiny sentence on mine saying 'have more sex' – we have all been there and life takes over a bit. Ted saw this on my vision board and asked, "Does that say have more sex? Are you going to leave Daddy?" It made me laugh as Ted thought that was the only way I would achieve having more sex!

If
The Plan

DOESN'T WORK,
CHANGE THE PLAN,
NOT THE GOAL.

May

Adam had agreed that I could look for a new car at the beginning of the year, but that had been put on hold. As the restrictions were now relaxing a little bit and the car showrooms started to reopen, I was on a mission – plus the funky smell was getting funkier. My house is spotless but my car is an embarrassment. If I'm going to be giving anyone a lift I need a good week's notice.

My car once went in for a service and the mechanic said, "Do you want me to get them to valet it while it's here?" "Yes, why not," I said, relived it would be one less thing I had to do. A couple of hours later I got a phone call saying they had refused to valet it. I was *even* paying for the valet. I haven't let it get that bad again, but it's close.

Getting Adam to agree anything to do with spending money is a challenge so I wasn't going to miss out on this opportunity of a new car.

Just to give you an idea of how I have learned to guide Adam in our spending, I had once wanted the bathroom redecorated but he wouldn't hear of it because nothing was broke in there. He didn't technically say 'no' though. So, he went to a festival with his mates. A nice break for him, I thought…and an opportunity for me! I sourced everything I needed for the bathroom renovation in secret and stored it all in a friend's garage up the road. I say in secret; it's just I didn't want him to worry about it – that's my story and I'm sticking to it.

On his way to the festival he rang me and put me on loudspeaker in the car. I chatted to him and his mates and just as I was finishing the conversation I quickly added, "Oh, just to let you know there's a tiler coming today, we're having the bathroom redone. Have an amazing time, love you, bye."

I know I'm childish but stuff like this makes me giggle. His mates thought this was hilarious, probably thankful that they weren't married to me. Adam didn't find it as funny. I got a few harsh text messages later that day but the tiler had started by then, hey ho.

As an aside, in one of Albie's pre-lockdown art lessons, he made me some bathroom accessories out of a pile of shite and stuck some glitter on them. He was so proud when he put them in the newly decorated bathroom. All my time spent on colour coding everything from towels to soap and now I had a toothbrush holder which was red, white and blue and looked like an elf had been sick – great! That's karma, I guess.

Back to the new car – Adam had only stipulated one thing and that was that my monthly payments had to be less than I was paying previously. What he didn't stipulate was by how much. Rookie error, Adam, rookie error.

On a drive out one Sunday afternoon (as that's all we could do around this time), I asked Adam if he wanted to go and see a car similar to my new car. His face went a little bit stern. "You've bought one?" I pretended to act like this wasn't a big deal. "Yes." I struggle with the whole 'let's discuss this first before you sign' things. But I'm getting better.

He went on to ask, "How much a month?" "It's less," I explained smugly. "How much less?" he persisted, knowing me too well. "Twelve pounds."

Strangely he didn't seem as pleased with this saving as I thought he would, and to say he blew his top was an understatement. It's not often Adam gets angry but when he does it makes me laugh. I've always been the same. I laugh through nerves and this didn't go down well.

He made lots of comments about us being in a partnership and that we should discuss these things but that just made me laugh more, which didn't help matters. I had to cover my mouth and try and squash my cheeks down to stop the laughter escaping.

So basically the Stinks saw Daddy being annoyed and angry and Mummy laughing uncontrollably. Great parenting skills, Irene.

LYNSEY-JAYNE'S STORY

I tried not to laugh, honest

I was once sat in the hairdressers minding my own business with a little old lady who was also waiting to be seen. The little old lady was reading a magazine and it dropped to the floor.

She bent down to pick it up, but as she was only little she fell forward and did a roly-poly across the salon floor. I couldn't breathe from laughing.

I realise I am going to hell.

Thankfully the lady hadn't had her hair done by that stage!

The last laugh was on me anyway. After a lot of emails to the car company I had my delivery date, so I went to We Buy Any Car and sold my car the morning my new car was arriving. Luckily, I had discovered what the funky smell was. There was a plated-up prawn cocktail from last Christmas Day in my boot. I had made sixteen to take to my mum's for starters and only arrived with fifteen. Oops.

After selling my car I returned home to find the car company had emailed me and they were having problems. The car wouldn't be ready for another four weeks.

They were also too busy to answer my frantic phone calls, conveniently.

I sent an email saying "Are you effin' joking?", but they didn't reply to that either. Obviously, my ability to complain in a professional and calm manner had come along in leaps and bounds since the incident with the babywear delivery.

I was now carless! I know in the grand scheme of things this isn't a big deal (especially when you couldn't really go anywhere much), but it was a big deal for me. Adam thought it was hilarious. Yes, I'm not laughing now, pal.

Thankfully a friend had a car that I could borrow, which was a life saver – well, if my weekly trip to Tesco saves lives?

MUM'S STORY
The Tesco incident

A text we received from my mum:

Did I tell you about the incident in Tesco's in Ireland when we were over last month?

Your dad and I called in to get some bits and pieces on our way to Phil's house. It was Saturday afternoon and the store was packed, but as we tried to find our way around the store we couldn't think straight for the awful rap music playing in the store on top note. It was Eminem at his worst and it was fiercely distracting, to the point where we were arguing looking for a toothbrush.

I kept trying to catch people's eye to do some proper eye rolling in disgust, when Eminem started effing and blinding, but everyone else seemed as distracted as we were. I couldn't decide whether to complain in the shop or write to Tesco's saying it wasn't suitable for a grocery store, never mind in an Irish Catholic town.

We headed for the till and were glad to be leaving. I went in my bag for my purse and noticed a light on my phone and Eminem playing on top note in my handbag. It was on my playlist since I accidentally ended up with Hannah's iTunes library.

We got such a shock and were so embarrassed we started laughing hysterically, leaning against a freezer with tears streaming down our faces only adding to the suspicion we were a pair of not rights!

Focusing on the positives, with my twelve pound a month saving, I could now buy more clothes and maybe get more of the house decorated. I just needed lockdown to be lifted fully so Adam could book a relaxing weekend away again.

Since the lockdown I have seriously increased my internet spending. Firstly, it was items to help with home-schooling – mini whiteboards, workbooks, face paints, big bouncy balls for the trampoline – then it moved on to clothes for me. Initially I ordered comfy clothes, which was now called loungewear. Pre-lockdown, this was called leggings and a baggy t-shirt/ pyjamas. Then I moved on to clothes that made you feel like you were going out somewhere nice, but in reality you just sat in the house in them. Then I had to re-order all of them again in a size bigger due to my fridge-raiding antics.

One night, through boredom, I ordered six headbands. This poor delivery guy risking his life so I could get six headbands. I'm sure I would have saved a lot of money and delivery men's lives if I had just bought a bottle of wine and be done with it.

I must remember to make sure Adam doesn't mistake the growing pile of clothes for rubbish, like he did last year. Over two hundred and fifty pounds' worth of clothes (that I was sending back) and he decided to do a 'tip' run. I couldn't really complain though, as the same month he had asked me to buy four tickets for a gig for him as he was on nights and would have been sleeping when the tickets were released. Buying gig tickets isn't something I generally do, so when I purchased four tickets for £400 I was impressed with myself. Non-refundable – that's fine! Adam wanted the tickets and I was sure he would be pleased with me too. It wasn't until he woke up and told me that the tickets should have been £25 a ticket that I realised I may have cocked up. Expensive month!

Well, you can't take it with you, but ideally we could do without hundreds of pounds' worth of mishaps like that again as I had further plans. As we were spending most of our time in our house and garden (and I knew the garden and bathroom were sorted), I became aware that the whole house needed redecorating. I think if you look hard enough you can always find something that needs doing, and once you see it you can't un-see it.

Adam did not see it. Well, he wouldn't. He's a big fan of the phrase 'if it ain't broke it doesn't need fixing.' But I'm more like 'if I get bored, decorate a room…or two.' I generally have to start sowing the seed early though, which goes against all my instincts to start pulling the wallpaper off the walls when I get the urge.

Adam likes to 'touch up'. (I'm talking about touching up the paint not touching up me – that comes later!) There is only so much touching up you can do without having to get the five-litre paint tub out. I had to start laying down hints. They would start subtle, as subtle as I could be anyway.

"Oh that wall is looking a bit grubby. I would hate for any of your mates to come round and see that." (it has to be *his* mates)

"It's a shame you work so hard or you would have time to do these jobs on the house." (said whilst rubbing his back)

"I think to help you out I will just get a price to see how much it would cost to redecorate the lounge." (said whilst nodding and smiling, like I am doing him a favour)

"You work long hours, it's not right that you should come home and start decorating." (said whilst shaking head with a concerned face)

Obviously, timing is key. You can't just blurt out all those lines in one go, you have to play it cool!

Other tips that can help your cause is to make some decent meals ready for as soon as they walk through the door (I struggle with this), have more sex (Adam will say I also struggle with this as he thinks he's funny), and to try to look interested in everything they say – don't worry, you only need to do this till they've agreed to said purchase.

If all these fail, then cry and explain the Feng Shui is all wrong in the house and you'd be less of a nagging wife if you could just sort it out. I haven't tried this one yet so please let me know if it works.

I realise now I am going to have to come up with some new plans as Adam will have read this and his guard will be up, so if you have any new ideas that have worked, let me know those too.

ITEMS ADAM THINKS ARE NECESSITIES	ITEMS I THINK ARE NECESSITIES
Redecorating when the wallpaper is falling off the wall	Redecorating when you're bored of the green that you insisted on twelve months ago when you needed your walls to make you feel calm and serene
Accessories - waste of money	All matching accessories to go with new colour on the same day you finish decorating, if not before
A car with four wheels, that gets you from A to B	A car no older than three years old, that still has that new car smell - yes, I know you can buy air fresheners for £3.99 that have that smell, but it's not the same
Hair clippers once every ten years	Hairdressing appointments, lashes done monthly and the odd Botox session
Buying one vinyl a month to add to his collection	When starting a new hobby, I need all the equipment, like yesterday, before I give up that hobby two weeks later
A couple of Pretty Green t-shirts come summertime	Five dresses, three pair of shoes, a pair of jeans and new pyjamas each month

Thankfully, Adam knows his limitations. In my very short first marriage, if I ever saw a piece of furniture I liked in a shop, my first husband would say, "I can make that for half the price." "Oh really. Let's just buy it, shall we, save you the trouble." I wonder could I have put that down as grounds for divorce? Although I suppose my infidelity probably tops that.

I often thought it would be handy being married to a decorator or a builder but I've got friends who are and I've seen now that their houses are the ones that get finished last.

So I don't know what the solution is. Maybe train to be a decorator myself? Hmmm…'Look for Effin' Rainbows Decorators' hasn't really got a ring to it. But I won't rule it out.

THREE THINGS I AM GRATEFUL FOR IN 2020:

• My nicely tiled bathroom.

• Saving twelve pound a month.

• Laughing even when it's inappropriate.

SELF-HELP TIP

Don't underestimate the power of laughter

There is even a laughter yoga now which I haven't tried…yet.

It feels good to laugh but it also has other benefits. Laughter strengthens your immune system, boosts your mood, diminishes pain and protects you from the damaging effects of stress. Even pretending to laugh or smile can have the same effect.

I read an article once about a woman who was diagnosed with cancer and instead of accepting medical treatment, she went home and watched hundreds of comedies and her cancer shrunk. Now, by no means am I telling anyone to do this, but I bet you didn't realise laughter can have such an impact on so many aspects of our lives.

Kids laugh all the time, but when you become an adult, life gets serious and laughing becomes rarer. I love a good laugh, especially one that keeps on giving. If Adam and I find something funny, we can chuckle for hours on that one thing.

Be so happy that when others look at you they become happy too.

My go-to TV program to make me laugh is You've been framed. I love it.

What doesn't **Kill You** MAKES YOU...THE PROUD OWNER OF A BUNCH OF COPING MECHANISMS AND AN ALARMINGLY DARK SENSE OF HUMOUR.

June

Hormones have featured quite heavily in our house this year, and for once I'm not the main culprit.

As we were spending more time in the house together, the dog and the cat were inside more too. The dog has decided he quite fancies the cat and tries to hump him every time the cat walks past. The poor cat has to gauge where the dog is before he even ventures into a room. He's a male and a cat, Barney. Leave him alone! I'm putting this down to Stockholm syndrome.

Stockholm syndrome must have affected Adam too, as every time I was doing menial tasks in the kitchen he would come behind me and hump me. Yes, Adam, not very helpful when I'm trying to take a chicken out of the oven – and no, that isn't a euphemism!

Obviously, a cook in the bag chicken – lockdown hadn't suddenly improved my culinary skills. However, the Stinks and I did make cupcakes a few times. I say cupcakes – that's what they were described as on the box – however, ours came out more like a cupcake traybake as we had overfilled the cupcake holders. But it's all a learning experience. For the Stinks and me.

When I complained about Adam's humping he would say "You'd be worried if I didn't do it." "Actually, no Adam, it would probably make my life a tad easier if you didn't honk my boobs and hump me while I attempted to cook the tea."

STACEY AND BRETT'S STORY

We're not alone

As we were both working from home and Charlie was being home-schooled, we spent a lot of time in each other's company.

One day when Charlie was online in his bedroom, 'Zoom'ing with his classmates, Brett and I felt a bit frisky. We decided as Charlie was occupied, it would be safe. We put a footstool behind the lounge door and started having a quickie.

I'm not very quiet when the moment takes me and was a bit louder than I should have been. Charlie ran downstairs and tried to open the lounge door, shouting, "Mum, Mum are you OK?"

We stopped. "Yes Charlie, I'm OK. Sorry, I was just messing with your dad."

"Ah OK." Charlie went back upstairs.

The moment had passed, so Brett and I went back to our work.

Later that evening, we were all sat watching *Star Wars* when one of the creatures on the screen started making a groaning sound. Charlie pipes up, "That's the same noise you were making earlier, Mummy."

He then proceeded to imitate the noise and pretty much did so all evening.

I bet you thought I was going to start to talk about *my* hormones, with me being forty-four and nearing the age of menopause, but nope, the highest hormone levels in my house at the moment are Ted's, the hormonal eight-year-old.

If you don't have boys or have grown up with boys, you will probably want to skip this chapter.

Ted is at the age where he wants to be grown up and treated like an adult but quite easily can have a paddy like a toddler. He can be sweet, angry, laughing and crying all in the space of five minutes. It's hard work and it's like having another me in the house.

I put it out there on social media – was this normal? Well, social media is where all the experts hang out. Most of the responses were from mums with children of similar ages and they were in agreement with me. This put my mind at rest somewhat.

One of the mums at Ted's school sent me a photo of a book she recommended as she had an older boy too and had been through this.

****WARNING****

Please look away now as I'm going to say a really horrendous word. On the front of the recommended book it says it covers everything from wet dreams to smegma! Uuuuurrrrrgghhhh. Is that really a word? Or if it is, is it a word to be plastered on the front of a book? I'm sure it is a very informative book, but I did wonder whether the author goes around saying, "I've written a book about wet dreams and smegma, have you read it?"

I know I shouldn't have typed it again there, but now it's there in black and white I can't stop typing it. Like when you say your first swear word as a teenager and you use it in every sentence. I'm going in for my fucking tea, I'll be back out fucking later. Bye fucking bye!

The fact that my sweet (most of the time) eight-year-old boy was going to be experiencing all this at his age made me want to stop time and wrap him up in cotton wool so those nasty hormones didn't get to him, but my job is to help him be the best version of himself and he needs those hormones to become a man – oh no! I want them to stay being my babies forever.

We met up with friends who have two boys at similar ages and our after dinner conversation turned to smegma, as it does. They couldn't believe it either and, just to prove my point, I googled it just to show them. Adam did tell me to stop talking about it in the restaurant, but I just couldn't. Did *you* know there's a word for the 'stuff' you find under the you-know-what?

It's even got a definition but you can google that yourself.

Ted has recently heard the words 'sexy' and 'sex'. I'd like to blame the other kids at school but he hasn't even been there. Ah, it might have been from my vision board (must remember to write in code from now on). He says these words quite a lot and we know it's to get a reaction out of us. He started saying "Ooh sexy Mummy", which we all laughed at but then I had to put my serious face on and say, "You've not to say that again, Ted."

He listened to me, for once, and changed the phrase. One evening going to bed, he said, "Shall me and Mummy have some sexy time?" Woooahhh!!! I didn't dare laugh at this one. Can you imagine him being back at school after lockdown?

Teacher: "So Ted, what did you do over lockdown?"

Ted: "Well, me and Mummy had some sexy time!"

Thankfully, he has stopped saying it now as we stopped reacting to it. Unfortunately, his new favourite phrase is 'Oh F word!' He knows he's not allowed to swear so he thought this would be acceptable. He was grounded – I know, how can you ground someone in lockdown? He's never been grounded before and he couldn't wait to tell his friends. Not the reaction I was looking for.

STUART'S STORY
The things they say

Me and Kavanagh used to watch an American series on Gold called *Hard Core Pawn*. It was our thing. The program was about a pawn shop in New York and its characters.

One night, Kavanagh had a sleepover at his mate Billy's. The next day I collected him and Billy's mum, Karen, came to the door to chat. Karen told me Kavanagh had been an angel as always.

It's always reassuring when they say that.

Then, Kavanagh looked at me and said, "Dad, can we go home and watch Hard Core Pawn tonight?"

I nearly fucking died!

BETHAN'S STORY
A spot of light reading

In my very early twenties, my friend and I decided to spend the day on the beach. After word got round, there ended up being a large group of us heading down for a day by the sea.

We all headed to the shop to buy supplies for our day and I grabbed a magazine to read whilst I was catching the rays. I picked up the first women's magazine I found as didn't want to waste sunbathing time.

Once there, we picked the best spot and laid out all our supplies, unfolded our towels and settled down.

I got my magazine out and opened the first page, which to my horror was a full frontal photo of a man lying all casual on a hay bale!

My heart beating wildly, I closed the magazine. Looking at the cover, it wasn't *New Woman* I had picked up in my haste, it was *For Women*.

So there was I, sat with all our friends, and I was reading porn!

Moving swiftly onto *my* hormones, which are far more important.

Since having babies, my hormones are like a little surprise each morning when I wake up. I've no idea who I'm going to be: happy Irene, crying Irene, don't-want-to-speak-to-anyone Irene. I could go on. I tell Adam it makes life interesting and he has the benefit of waking up with a different woman each morning. He's not convinced.

I've recently learned about the term 'perimenopause'. I didn't know there was even such a thing. Apparently, it's that lovely time when you have loads of symptoms BEFORE your menopause. So basically, I went through puberty with acne, had three pregnancies with acne, then perimenopause with acne, so I think I've had about three days blemish-free in my life.

In 'proper' terminology, perimenopause means 'around menopause' and refers to the time during which your body makes the natural transition to menopause, marking the end of your reproductive years. Sometimes I think ignorance is bliss and the more you read about the symptoms, the more you get the symptoms.

When I was younger I did think that I would have loads of children, but that wasn't to be. Pregnancy didn't really suit me. I didn't flourish or bloom. I got sepsis, post-natal depression and my body failed one of my babies.

We have our work cut out with the two Stinks and thought that was it for reproduction in our house. But suddenly, when that decision is close to being taken away, it makes you think. Could I just manage one more? I think I could. I heard so much about lockdown babies and how there would be a baby boom. I was seriously considering it and the Stinks were growing up quickly. You couldn't have too big of an age gap – but saying that, there is twenty years between me and my younger sister, Hannah, and we love each other. My mum is a bit knackered though! I did Google it but the chances of having a spontaneous pregnancy at forty-four years of age was zero. How was I going to get that one past Adam? I was good but not that good.

Adam, on the other hand, categorically says no. I know I don't usual listen to Adam, but as this is more than just tiling the bathroom or buying a car, I think I have to accept we are done.

Having said all that, if you've read my first book, you will know I always thought I would have girls. It would be nice to have a daughter. I can even imagine how she looks: chubby cheeks and curly hair. It would be comforting to have someone to share all my womenly issues.

CAROL'S STORY
Removing all evidence

When my daughter first started her periods we had a talk about all the things she needed to know. However, she must have felt so embarrassed putting her pads in the bin that she would just toss them out of her bathroom window instead.

Never to be seen again apparently...

That was until the water board knocked on the door to report the street was flooded...and there we found a nice collection of old pads blocking the grid right under her bathroom window.

I didn't have Ted till I was thirty-six so was classed as an older mum. By the time I got round to having Albie two years later, I was practically ancient. I do wonder if I had met Adam sooner whether would we have a tribe by now and would it have been as hard. I do think the biggest leap is from having one child to having two. From there on in, you don't really notice the extra bodies in the house. But hey, that's not me talking from experience. I'll never know.

And as I always say, everything happens for a reason and I am happy with my lot.

I don't know if it was hormones or lockdown or a combination of both, but around this time I became overwhelmed by social media and life in general. I was starting to struggle.

After having joined many groups to help me during lockdown, it slowly dawned on me that it was these groups that were the reason I was feeling anxious. I would wake up in a morning and before even opening my eyes I would feel the anxiety in my chest. It was a feeling of dread but I didn't know what I was dreading. I would instinctively look at my phone and scroll through social media. Everyone in these groups seemed to have their shit together and it made me feel like I was inadequate. I should be doing all these amazing things and making the most out of lockdown, but I was just coasting.

Looking back on this and talking with a friend recently, she was incredulous and said, "What the heck are you talking about? You've written a book and published it, recovered from brain surgery and given up alcohol. How can you say you've just been coasting?" I guess it is all a matter of perspective and how we do ourselves down.

Anxiety is a word I had never heard about ten years ago but now it's everywhere. Some anxiety is a good thing, it's part of your flight or flight mode. I remember as a uniformed police officer on the beat, when I had to put my blue sirens on, the feeling I would get in my stomach. This was the adrenaline being released in my body and I loved that feeling. Some anxiety is good for your body.

When I released my first book, I remember looking at my Fitbit and my heart rate was unusually high; it was exciting. Wow, could I actually burn calories sat on my arse writing and publishing another book? That's why I'm writing this one – research purposes.

However, when you wake up in a morning and you are feeling anxious for no reason, that isn't healthy. Because of this, I decided to have a social media break and go back to basics like reading a book (I knew a good one!), watching rubbish TV, relaxing in a bath, meditation, anything just to help me switch off at night.

Generally, just as I had settled myself down for the night, had my bath, finished my meditations, I would lie there waiting for sleep to happen, and then Boom, would get my best ideas for my writing. Then in the morning, I would completely forget them. (Sorry, this book would have been far funnier if I could have remembered my night time paragraphs.)

To combat this loss of ground-breaking ideas, I resorted to having a pen and paper at the side of my bed. But that didn't help, because one thought lead to another and I would be writing a chapter at 2am!

There was also an element of practising what I preached. I had been telling Ted that if his emotions became all mixed up, to take himself off to have a bath or do something relaxing. However, it's easier giving advice to someone else rather than doing it yourself.

Due to this feeling of anxiety in a morning, I would overthink everything throughout the day. I felt like I was failing in all areas. In my mind, I was a failure as a writer, a failure compared to everyone who was spending lockdown learning a new language or baking banana bread, a failure as a wife and a failure as a mother. I also felt I was a failure keeping the Stinks off school. Adam and I didn't anticipate it would be this long and when one of you is struggling, it has a knock-on effect for the whole family.

In a state of panic late one night, I emailed the school and asked please, please, please can the Stinks (referred to by their actual names in the email) come back to school. This option was always available with us being key workers, so thankfully they agreed. The Stinks went back three days a week. And breathe…

But then I felt like a failure sending them in. I just couldn't win in my head.

We are great at dishing out the advice but we struggle to do it ourselves.

THREE THINGS I AM GRATEFUL FOR IN 2020:

• Hormones are only ever a phase.

• My body safely bringing me my two Stinks.

• Adam isn't hormonal too, as one or both of us
would be in prison (probably me),
divorced or dead (probably Adam).

KRISTINA'S STORY
The 'talk'

Bella was about 3 years old at the time, and being a curious child she burst into the bedroom after going to the toilet one day and announced she had ripped a hole! She quickly lay on the floor, legs akimbo and pointed worriedly at her vulva.

Now, I'm not a squeamish mum and it takes a lot to embarrass me. So in the true spirit of motherhood, I rolled my proverbial sleeves up and tackled her concern with science. After all, I thought, we call an arm an arm - she needs to know the name for her body and to make up words would cause more problems later down the line.

So we had the chat.

Girls have vaginas and boys have a penis.

I was pretty proud, it was a very grown-up chat and even the hubby got involved! We pointed out that Grandad (my dad) had a penis; what a wonderful chat about my dad's cock that was! Never again to be spoken about (except now). And that Auntie Nicola would have a vagina. All good. Boxed off.

→

But just to be sure, I messaged EVERY family member we would be seeing that week to warn them in case my three-year-old blurted out about her vagina or their penis! "Please don't go red-faced!"

Amazingly, it was not mentioned again. Excellent. What a mum win! Look how you handled that, you fantastical beast of a woman you!

Three weeks later we were sat waiting for a table at Nandos; Bella was playing with her Barbie doll when an unsuspecting elderly couple sat down by her.

"Oh!" The lovely little old lady exclaimed at Bella's Barbie, "Your dolly has no pants on!"

Without missing a beat, Bella looked squarely at this woman and informed her, "Girls have a bagina and boys have pennies."

I had no words for this confused and horrified little lady. I have never wanted the ground to swallow me up so much. I'm so sorry.

SELF-HELP TIP

Take your own advice.

We're all good at dishing out advice, but taking that advice ourselves is another matter. I was telling Ted to do all those activities that would help his hormones - and yet wasn't taking my own advice. I could use that too. My hormones and I have been together for over thirty years and I know what helps and what doesn't, so I need to implement these things rather than accepting moody arse Irene when she comes along.

Hormonal feelings can creep up and bite you on the arse and you have no clue what has happened or where they have come from.

Try journaling your feelings. Days when you are feeling low, days when you are tired for no reason. Days when you feel good for no reason. You don't have to write *War and Peace*; use an emoji if that helps.

Also look back at how far you've come. We can all be guilty of being focused on what we haven't acheieved as opposed to looking at what we have achieved. Write these wins down and congratulate yourself on them.

There will be a pattern to your feelings, and the next month try to preempt those dips. It can be something as simple as staying off your phone for a day or going for a walk on your own. Don't undervalue a trip to Tesco's alone.

Look at the foods you're eating around your bad days. Did you have three chocolate bars for tea or a bottle of wine? There are so many things that affect our hormones that we can control.

We can't all diary in a spa day (or afford it even), but we can make some time for ourselves that doesn't cost anything.

Saying that you need a bit of space is not failing, it's effin' winning, and I know through experience, your family will thank you for taking a bit of time out and coming back fresher.

Once you've found 'that thing' that helps you and your hormones, make that thing a habit.

I Thought

I WAS HAVING A
HOT FLUSH THIS MORNING,
THEN I REALISED
MY BOOBS WERE
IN MY BREW!

July

All of our holidays had been cancelled. To be honest, that didn't seem as bad as I thought it would as nobody was going on any holidays. So it wasn't like we were going to be seeing everyone's holiday snaps on social media. Everyone was in the same boat. (or not, as the case was.)

We'd had some reprieve with the Stinks going to school for three days a week, but the summer holidays were now upon us.

At least we didn't have the added pressure of home-schooling, although it did cross my mind that if I was a good parent I should carry on with it, to catch up some of what they missed out on. But thankfully that was just a fleeting thought.

Adam and I were working shifts – albeit mine were from home. When I worked out our shift patterns, I noticed that we had three days which coincided where we were all off at the same time. We checked out what we were allowed to do given the travel restrictions, etc. and booked some day trips.

We always go to Southport. I've no idea why, but that is our 'go to' day trip out. It was Ted's first ever day out when he was a baby and I posted photos on social media showing how I was acing it, but looking back now, I can still see the 'what the f**k am I doing' look in my eyes. I remember Ted screaming, wanting to be fed when we were on our way home in the car, and me crying because Adam couldn't find anywhere to stop so I could feed him. Aw, memories.

However, we spent a lovely blustery day at Southport for our 2020 holidays, and for the next couple of days we booked the Crocky trail and a Sunflower maze for our family entertainment.

I've never been to the Crocky trail, but it's been there years apparently – and to be honest, it looked like it's been there years, but it was so much fun. We had proper belly laughs, all four of us. It felt like such a long time since we had had belly laughs, and it was just what we needed.

As an over-cautious parent, I did get a bit panicky when Ted was coming down one of the rickety slides. I get events happening in my head, a bit like *Final Destination*. After Albie was born, I had post-natal depression and one of the main things I was doing was catastrophising things and seeing things in my head all leading to Albie dying. I hate even saying that now, but that's the way my head was working at the time. If Albie coughed, I would think, 'Right, this is it, this is how he is going to die.' Thankfully, most of that has gone, but I still get little snippets popping back up and this was one of these times.

In my head I could see Ted's long hair getting caught on the slide as he was coming down. I can't even write the sequence of events that followed in my brain. I had to turn away. I asked Adam if these thoughts were normal and he said, "No." Okay then, just me.

It takes a conscious effort to make myself stop thinking these thoughts and then I can enjoy the moment, like all the other 'normal' parents out there.

There was one slide where you stood on ledge and there was a young lad there who pulled a lever and the floor was swiped away from under your feet and you went hurtling down. Ted wanted to go on it and I wanted to show him that he can do anything if he puts his mind to it. We both excitedly ran up the rickety wooden stairs, Ted stalling slightly once at the top.

My heart broke when I saw his face, he was petrified. I reassured him and explained how good he would feel once he did it. His eyes were all wide, full of fear, and he just kept looking at me and trying to hold my hand. Events like this don't happen often and I thought to myself, right Irene, this is a pivotal moment in Ted's life, he's looking at you for guidance and support, show him that you are there for him and that he can achieve anything in life with his mum by his side. I said to him, "Honestly Ted, you're going to be fi…Hoooollllyyyy Shhhhiiiitttt!" The floor disappeared and I screamed like a banshee all the way down!

Ted got back up on his feet laughing and running to go on again. I couldn't stand, my legs were shaking that much. Ted also had to be taught the lesson that you can have too much of a good thing, and for that moment I was choosing that lesson. Daddy's turn.

The Sunflower maze was a lot calmer. The lads struggled with the fact that they couldn't pull out a sunflower to whip each other, but all in all we had a good day. It had been raining heavily the day before we arrived. (Isn't that always the same – school term time, glorious sunshine, summer holidays, torrential rain?) Adam had chosen to wear white pumps. You always see one! Suffice to say, they weren't white when we exited the maze.

Whilst walking out of the maze I got a phone call from my boss. "Hi Irene, where are you?" "I'm at the Sunflower Maze." "Ah right, you do know you should be working today and yesterday for that matter?" "Shit!"

Looks like I was working the weekend then. That was our 2020 summer holidays done. Back to work.

Before lockdown, alongside my day job (when I bothered to log on – only kidding, Boss!) I had started networking to market myself and my book. Networking was something that filled me with dread at first. Walking into a room and speaking to a room full of strangers was scary. I was OK once I was seated, but the whole making small talk with someone you had never met or have any idea of who they were filled me with apprehension.

It's funny, because at face-to-face events (remember those?) you'd notice people who you thought were your kind of people at first glance, and mostly those feelings were right. For me, it boils down to things like: Have they made eye contact with me? Do they have an open stance? And as shallow as it sounds, the clothes they are wearing. I'm not a snob or anything, but if someone is suited and booted, looking all professional and as though they know what they are talking about, I would be wondering what we would have in common. That says more about me than them though! I would gravitate more to the lady who walked in with her dress tucked into her knickers. I would think, yes, that's my kind of woman.

On my first few times going to these events, I would walk in with my head down, grab a brew (making no eye contact with anyone), find my seat and probably sit with my arms crossed. Something I needed to work on maybe?

I found a lovely networking group which was local to me and I had got to know a few people. The organiser knew I had wanted to try my hand at public speaking. This was something that was way out of my comfort zone – it has been a major fear of mine since reading out the words 'river Thames' in primary school (I read it how it is spelt, pronouncing the 'th' of 'Thames' as you would say 'thought') and all the other children in the class laughed at me. I would have laughed too if I was bright enough to realise. But that moment has stuck with me.

Now I was in a place where I wanted to try new things and I now knew how to say Thames – however it never cropped up in my talks. (must figure out how to squeeze that one in, show off my new-found skill)

I wanted to speak out about my story and having Dusty for two reasons:

    1) saying Dusty's name as often as I could validated that he existed and he was my son, and

    2) if I could help someone going through similar circumstances and show them there is light at the end of the tunnel, speaking out could help them and in turn that would help me too.

The first time I spoke in front of a group of people I didn't know, it would be fair to say I was shitting myself. I had it planned weeks in advance; I had practised it on Adam on numerous occasions, to the point which I think he knew it better than I did. I didn't want to know it word perfect so I bought some pretty rainbow (why not?) bullet point cards I could use as prompts.

On the day, I picked a friendly face in the audience and went for it. I spoke so fast I'm not sure everyone (or anyone) could keep up, and once I started I couldn't stop. Forgetting about the cards in my shaky hands, I went off on a tangent, which you may have noticed I have form for. But I enjoyed it. I felt elated at the end that I hadn't frozen or been sick whilst stood in front of everyone – so all in all, I was taking that as a success.

I was at the stage where I was enjoying public speaking. I still got that nervous adrenaline feeling in my stomach before any event but now that spurred me on.

Through being brave and standing up, telling them my story, I had found people within the networking community that I would gravitate to as they had similar stories. We forged friendships based on our own separate experiences.

One of those people I met was Emma. I was speaking at Emma's local networking event and she had only decided to go at the last minute. As I was talking, I saw that Emma was crying. My story is a bit sad but Emma was crying real tears and I knew what I was saying about Dusty had happened to her. When I finished a talk, I generally gave away one of my books, and usually it was a case of pulling a name out of a hat. On this day it was Emma's name. As I gave Emma the book, we hugged – not the kind of brief hug you give someone you don't know very well, a real heartfelt hug. I knew then that we had met for a reason.

EMMA'S STORY

Lillie

Irene started talking and I was enjoying her story. Unbeknown to me was what was to come next. She went on to speak about Dusty and it dragged me back to when Lillie was born. I started feeling all the pain, hurt and anger from when I was losing her. Irene was saying exactly how I felt at the time... She knows, she's been there... Oh my gosh..! Keep it in, Emma, this is Irene's moment. You need to keep strong, so she doesn't get upset. I thought, 'I hope she can't see me. She's so strong.'

I couldn't hold back my tears and I started sobbing – you know, the noisy type, when you get a pain in your throat and struggle to swallow. I was trying my best to stop myself, but the emotional pain hit me like a bus.

For me, it was 24 ½ weeks pregnant, no complications and suddenly, my little girl was coming. I knew she was a girl. I was impatient and had to find out. I had no control of what happened that day. I was rushed to Blackburn hospital to be told she was coming. Somehow I knew the worst was going to happen. I was given all kinds of drugs for Lillie-Beth, to prepare her for birth as her lungs would be too undeveloped to breathe on her own.

The hospital had to send me to Preston as there just wasn't any special beds or equipment for Lillie if she came early. I stayed in bed for two days, where all the pains and signs of labour had stopped. As there were no signs of the labour continuing, my nurse said I could have a walk about. My hubby, Chris, went home for some things and I braved getting up. I must admit, I was scared to get moving again, as I hadn't been fully checked by a doctor and I was just unsure if things were safe. Anyway, I trusted them and got up and waddled to the toilet, afraid to open my legs even a little bit to walk. Whilst on the loo I felt a sudden gush! What the hell? Lillie was born in the bloody toilet... I stretched and struggled to open the door and scream for help. The emergency cord was typically wrapped round the shower, out of reach. Without having time to think, I scooped Lillie up. Nurses rushed in and she was rushed away. Where's Lillie gone? What's happened? Is she alive?

Back in the networking room, hearing Irene tell her story, I kept jumping me back to this part of my memory. I recognised Irene's pain for Dusty. I didn't know what to do or think, sat there with other female businesswomen around me. Thinking I wasn't professional if I wasn't strong! That had gone out the window; I was a mess!

Calming down a little, I realised that there was someone else who'd shared what had happened to me. I know it's quite common, but having the potential to connect with someone about my traumatic experience would mean a lot.

'How was Lillie?' I hear you ask. She was doing so well for a few days, but then we had some bad news that her bowel had ruptured and she needed surgery. In Manchester! "Oh God, please no. This is when we are going to lose her!" She was blue-lighted in an ambulance, so we had to drive ourselves and meet them at the hospital, so frightened and unaware of what was going to happen. We got to the hospital and whilst in the lift to go to her new ward, the lift stopped, the alarms went off and we were stuck. How much more tense could this day be? Lillie got caught up in the drama, but she had her own power supply for her cot, so she was fine. She got her place on the ward and we got shown a room for us.

We had a meeting with a consultant, who was going through her notes from the last two weeks, and he said she had less than 10% chance of surviving this operation and it being successful. Hubby had to call our parents, update them and tell them to come and see her as she may not survive. Lillie was taken for her operation and we went to our room, where we waited and waited for hours. At 11pm we got a knock on the door. The nurse said she had survived and had done so well. "Bloody hell, our little girl is a fighter, she may get through this. There is hope."

A week passed and she was doing great. We were washing her, changing her nappies and chatting with her every minute. She was probably sick of me singing and telling her stories of her brother Cameron, who was five. He loved her and brought her things every visit. He drew her a sheep which he placed in her cot to keep her safe, and he designed her nursery at the childminders one day. Somehow at the small age, he sort of understood what was happening and that she was poorly, but he still made us smile when he was with us. We stayed at the hospital to be with Lillie, so Cameron was at Grandma's & Grandad's, which we felt so guilty about. But he was fine and loving it. 😔

We had some heart-breaking news: Lillie's bowel had burst again but further down, so more surgery was needed. Imagine our thoughts: "There's no way she can survive another operation, she's not strong enough and still recovering from the last one." Well guess what... our girl pulled through and was doing well at just three weeks old.

Hubby had bought her a little pink elephant, called Ellie. He placed it in her cot to keep her safe and to have some company when we were in bed or nipping home to see Cameron. The feeling knowing you want to be with your daughter who's fighting for her life as well as your five-year-old son who needs you too was a horrendous feeling, but we had to juggle everything to do the right thing for all of us.

Lillie was doing so well and gaining weight and we were just so proud of her. The signs were good but then she showed signs of other conditions starting. When Lillie was born, she banged her head and this caused brain haemorrhages. She had two of them at stage 3. So, we were prepared for the fact that she will be disabled due to the pressure on her brain. But we really didn't care. She was fighting for us, so we were fighting for her.

We spent nearly every minute with her, learning how to clean her tubes, listening to the machines. (Oh god, how I hate that sound now) It was becoming normal, but we had hope!

We spent weeks tending to Lillie, spending lots of time with her, becoming her nurses. Family and friends visited with gifts and cards. Her special elephant teddy was in her cot all the time. We tried to have meals out but couldn't speak to each other and just ended up rushing back to the hospital to be close to her. Chris even tried to return to work, as he'd used up his paternity leave. He didn't work for long.

Our hope was shattered when we were advised Lillie had contracted meningitis in and around her brain - she just wasn't going to survive. We could tell she had got worse and even her medication wasn't stopping the pain for her. We had two options, to let her pass away naturally or turn off her machine. What a decision to have to make as a parent! But we could see how much pain she was in and we chose to take her to a quiet room and cuddle her as she passed away.

We held Lillie for hours, and when our parents arrived, we gave them time with her, to say their goodbyes. This was so hard for us all, but also very calming. I know that sounds strange, but being able to all hold her and chat with family about a few normal things was strangely soothing. We left the hospital later with a lovely little box with her blankets, hats, nappies (clean ones, of course) and all her little wires and cards the nurses had gathered for us. Walking out of the hospital was the hardest thing I have had to do, leaving my little girl alone and all I had was this box.

I love this box and if my house were on fire, this is what I would grab. Obviously, the boys too, but they are grown up, so I know they'd be there with me. 'Lillie elephant' now comes on holidays and trips with us. The boys slept with her for many years, which I loved. I say the boys, as I had

Ollie one year after Lillie. We have always talked and included Lillie. He was very close with her and this is why he slept with her for years.

Once Lillie's tubes were removed, the nurse wanted to take a pic of her. I refused at first and was so mad. "Why would I want a picture of my baby who had passed away?" But the nurse insisted and I'm so glad she did now. Ollie looks just like her and I know this because I have this picture without all her tubes, I can see them both together.

So, this is Lillie's story. Although she isn't here today physically, she's definitely with us in spirit and we make memories as a family, all together. Lillie is part of our Company, CoverMyBubble, she's our rainbow covering people with the right protection, so every day I get to include her in my life more. But she touches other people lives now too, just like Dusty does. 😊

So, you now know my story and why on that special day I connected with the most wonderful lady, Irene Wignall. Irene sharing her story helped me so much. I have spoken up more about Lillie and helped other people along the way too.

Irene's story had a massive impact on my life and she gave me the courage to read Lillie's diary. I hadn't read it for over twelve years. Each day, for thirty days we wrote how Lillie was, how we were feeling, and what was going on in our crazy world. Irene has helped me read seven days so far and one day – when we can blooming meet up that is (Lockdown 2020) – we may read more together. I'm just not strong enough yet.

With love, Lillie Pops xxx

This is why I talk and write about Dusty and other events in my life. Talking about your difficulties can have such a massive impact on other people, some you hear about, others you don't.

Without taking the courage to speak at these networking events, I would have never met Emma. I am a big believer in fate and truly believe everything happens for a reason.

All my networking was then transferred to online events. I'm not as keen on the online events as they lack the personal touch, but I persevered as this was all we had at the moment. I'd prep my top half before the Zoom, makeup on, hair done, fake tan on face, neck and arms. PJ's on the bottom half, legs unshaven, fluffy socks on.

I have always tried to be girly, but it doesn't come naturally, no matter what tan I use or what latex gloves or amazing mitts I use to apply it. I always have some random tanned thumb or finger. Adam said to me the other day, "I didn't know you had a birthmark on your stomach." "I don't, that's just a random bit of fake tan that must have flicked off my arm."

I would never (knowingly) use fake tan on my stomach because no one outside my house is ever going to see that area – apart from a whole group of strangers in Iceland, that is! Or if I was unconscious and they were conducting CPR – and then I would hope they were concentrating on the CPR rather than my bad tan lines.

First impressions were harder to gauge on Zoom events. You see, a lot of us have a resting bitch face – I have one, it's normal. It's not natural to smile the whole way through a Zoom call because then you're giving off a whole different vibe! Here's Johnny!

Now, I found myself looking at my face more than I usually did, as online meetings were a regular occurrence and going nowhere soon (bit like me!). Because of this, I focused more time on analysing my wrinkles/laughter lines – as I had only had one bout of belly laughs this year, I think the ratio was more like 80% wrinkles: 20% laughter lines. I had seen an advertisement requesting a model to trial out a new technique in a local salon, and as my face was the only thing now on show, I thought this was perfect timing. It was also free of charge so Adam couldn't moan at this one.

I submitted my interest and a photo and I was selected. I'm not sure if that was a compliment or not? I didn't really know what I'd signed up to but I knew it should get rid of some wrinkles. It did say I needed a week's downtime. Well, I wasn't going anywhere soon so it was the ideal time.

Once at the salon they applied numbing cream on my face before the treatment began and sat me down in the waiting room. I could hear another woman having the treatment done in the other room. It seemed to come to an abrupt end from what I heard but I was more concerned about what was in store for me rather than the other woman.

The treatment was tiny burn marks around my eyes, forehead and cheeks. I could literally smell my skin burning. I had the treatment. It hurt. It hurt a lot. It hurt more than brain surgery!

I was lying on the bed willing them to stop. I nearly said just effin' leave the left hand side, I'll just make sure I always look at people using my right side only, but I couldn't chicken out. I'm a grown woman, for God's sake! I had put myself forward for this and it was the first and probably only time I would be classed as a model. When they finished, they casually told me the woman prior to me had walked out halfway through. Well, if I'd have known that I wouldn't have been lying there.

As I drove away I sneaked a peek in the rear view mirror. Oh my God, how was I going to explain this to Adam? I looked like something out of Avatar. I had tiny burns all over my eye lids, underneath my eyes and around my forehead and I still smelt a bit too. Even now, I still get the whiff of burnt flesh today if the wind blows in a certain direction!

Adam has a thing about tiny holes, it's called trypophobia. He can't stand the sight of tiny holes, even in a crumpet. Well, a crumpet face was going to be staring him for the next week.

I had to tell the Stinks I'd had an allergic reaction and it was nothing to worry about. Adam looked at me and gagged. Not the reaction I want from my husband when he looks at me. Every time he turned to talk to me, he gagged again, and it took a couple of days for that to stop. I had a couple of Zoom meetings that week but I moved around loads and sat as far from the camera as possible. I probably looked like I was on speed. Very professional, Irene.

Thankfully it calmed down and I had fresh skin underneath. But I'll put that up there with one of life's lessons which I probably won't learn from. So if anyone would like a model to trial out any wrinkle reducing treatment for free, I'm your woman.

HEATHER'S STORY
The beautiful bridesmaid

It was my friend's wedding and I was a bridesmaid.

I went to have a spray tan and eyebrow and eyelash tinting the day before the wedding. Unfortunately, the salon that I went to didn't advise me that you weren't supposed to have both these treatments done on the same day; you are supposed to leave a few days between. Anyway, I got home and realised that I had bright orange eyebrows.

The makeup artist tried her best to correct it for the wedding the next day, but let's just say on the wedding photos I'm not hard to identify!

During one of my networking Zooms, I explained that I wanted my first book to be on television. Why not dream big? Through another lady in the meeting, I was introduced to a TV producer who loved the book and said she'd get back to me. That would be amazing! I knew I had to play it cool and keep it to myself. That would be fine as I have form for keeping things to myself. Not.

I had a really good feeling about this. Amongst all the chaos of 2020, it really was going to be our year.

A couple of weeks later I received a formal letter of understanding and a plan of what was going to happen. The production company wanted to get a scriptwriter on board and I would become a co-writer of the show. It would be based on my book and my life. I would be involved in casting the characters and be an advisor on the show. Move over Peter Kay. I was shaking when I read the email and actually crying through excitement. I could not believe this was going to happen to me, to us. We all jumped around the front room, dancing and cheering.

Adam and I discussed who would play our roles. I thought Michelle Keagan would be perfect for my character, because of our many similarities (northern and female). Adam picked Jason Statham. Again, resounding similarities (bald and male). I'd discuss these potential actors further with the production company next time I spoke to them.

This gave me so much confidence that someone else had faith in our dreams.

I updated my vision board and printed off a photo of a BAFTA award. I started looking at BAFTA dresses online. None of the now humongous pile of new 'lounge' clothes were going to cut it. I lay in bed at night visualising the awards ceremony. "And the winner of best newcomer and funniest person in the business…drum roll…Irene Wignall." I'd turn and kiss Adam (an air kiss on both sides obviously) as everyone stood up to applaud me.

I'd have to practise walking in heels again – stick that on my 'to do' list.

I do know I'm odd, but I actually did visualise all this!

Whilst this was all going on in the background, I was interviewed a couple of times on Facebook lives by different groups. (The ones that I had unfollowed earlier and when I felt more balanced re-followed.) It was all practice for *This Morning* with Holly and Phillip. I never mentioned the TV production company but it was right there on the tip of my tongue, dying to come out.

I try to add some humour into any interviews as that's what I'm about. It was a bit unnerving when I gave a punch line on one interview and the interviewee was glaring at me, unblinking. What was staring back at me was not the laughing face I expected, but a scary face which looked like a cat's arse. I just ended up laughing at my own joke in a really awkward way until the screen unfroze.

KERI'S STORY

My Zoom co-star

I had been working from home and attending all my work meetings via Zoom.

I made sure that that corner of the room behind me on Zoom was spotless. I even called it the Zoom corner and told Isla that none of her toys could go into that space.

Isla is an only child and very good at entertaining herself when she needs to.

One of my Zoom meetings went on for quite a while, and as no one else on the call was doubling up as childcare as well as work, no one else was in a rush to end the call.

Isla had been very good, being quiet throughout, playing with her Lol dolls, but she then came bursting in the room shouting, "Mummy, Mummy, I've had a poo and I've wiped my bum myself. Look."

To my horror, she held up a piece of toilet roll with poo smeared all over it, a big grin plastered across her face, with her tights and knickers at her ankles.

I tried to push her and the toilet roll from the view of the camera and instead wiped shit all over my hand. Strangely, the meeting wrapped up quickly after that.

One Zoom call, Albie refused to leave me alone so I spent the whole time chatting with a pair of feet resting on my shoulders. Don't they say 'never work with kids and animals'? Now I'm in the business, Dahling, I know what I'm talking about when it comes to the media!

THREE THINGS I AM GRATEFUL FOR IN 2020:

- Ted's braveness (not mine).

- Having a flexible boss.

- Meeting Emma.

SELF-HELP TIP
Visualisation.

This is different from your vision board. It's really quite simple – which is good, as I like simple... love you, Adam!

You sit in a comfortable position, close your eyes and imagine. We have probably all done this as a kid, but we seem to lose the art of imagination the older we get.

You imagine your goal in as much detail as you can. Imagine it as though you are already doing it. Imagine the smells, the sounds, how it makes you feel inside, even down to details of what you are wearing at the time.

I'll tell you one of mine – I've told you everything (Well, half of the year anyway, there's still a point in finishing the book!), so no point in being shy now.

I imagine driving into my driveway (double driveway) of my double-fronted house, nothing too grand. I get out of my car. I'm happy sticking with my new car but upgrade to a leather interior. I can smell the leather.

I'm in gym gear as I have been to the gym and picked up some shopping on my way home. I'm looking pretty hot in my gym gear and don't need to wear an oversized t-shirt to hide my arse.

I open the door and my hallway smells fresh, not of farts like it does now. To my left is the living room and to my right is my office. My office has awards and photos with celebrities adorning the walls. At the bottom of the hall is the kitchen.

I walk into the kitchen, which is an open plan kitchen, dining, and family area. Ted and Albie are at the dining table doing their homework and Adam is sat on the sofa sorting out his podcast.

The dog and the cat are no longer humping and the bi-fold doors are open to let in the sunshine.

I can smell fresh coffee (none of us drink coffee but I like the smell) as I place the shopping on the kitchen island and take out the microwave meals for our tea! (Well, I am a realist!)

We all chat about how good our days have been.

Now, I know that the Stinks are probably not going to sit and do homework through choice and the dog will probably still be humping the cat. There will be probably be muddy paw prints on the tiled floors as the bi-fold doors are open and it's been raining – but it's my imagination. If you are going to do it, you may as well go big.

The idea behind the technique of visualising yourself achieving your goals is that it works by getting your mind and body ready for what you want to happen. A bit like exercise, the more you work on a muscle, the stronger it becomes. Going into as much detail as possible helps with that. There's no point in doing a half-arsed sit up – that won't achieve a six pack alone. You need to really focus on the details, the sounds, the smells, what you can see, and make it as real in your head as possible. It's also been proven scientifically that it can work but you need to believe it. Only five to ten minutes a day can radically improve your life. No harm in trying, eh?

If your
Dreams
DON'T SCARE YOU,
THEY AREN'T BIG ENOUGH...

...OH, AND NEVER WORK
WITH KIDS OR ANIMALS!

August

When I wrote my previous book (hark at me!) I was just at one year sober. That was the challenge I had set myself – one year, no beer. But in that one year I had achieved so much, so what did I want to do now?

It was so much easier to explain to people I wasn't drinking because I was doing a year challenge, it was like a safety net, but now that was over.

My decision was never to go tee total forever, but I just can't imagine what would have to happen to make me change my mind as the positives definitely outweigh the negatives. The negatives in my case were living in a foggy haze. I wasn't an alcoholic but I was becoming dependant on alcohol to help me through any emotions, from feelings of happiness all the way through to the feelings of grief. I no longer had a happy relationship with alcohol and I hated being the one out of the family that fell into the Christmas tree Christmas day evening, so I knew something needed to change.

At the time, I thought about maybe just drinking on odd occasions once my one year was up, but how would I work out which occasion is that important that warrants me having a glass of wine more than another? That one glass of wine would invariably lead to another, being drunk, talking shit and then falling over. We all know habits take a long time to break but it's annoyingly very easy to fall back into an old habit.

Ideally, I would like to maybe have one glass whilst out for a meal (if we can ever go out again) or a couple on a night out. But then that brings about my mind being consumed with thoughts of alcohol and I just wanted to stop thinking about alcohol full stop. As I had already made the decision to quit, should I not just stick to that?

As I'm writing this book, I have hit the two-year mark and I honestly think that's me done forever with alcohol. I recently had a conversation with Adam where I'd decided that when I am a granny I will start drinking again, a glass of sherry or two at Christmas time. I don't know why this is my plan, but Adam just nodded, as he does.

If you are like me, spending too much time thinking about alcohol – Am I drinking too much? Should I stick to drinking shorts? Should I only drink on weekends? Should I only drink when I'm Out, Out? Should I have this third tequila? – then you are wasting way too much energy and head space on alcohol. When you're not drinking it, you're recovering from the effects of it, and once recovered you are then thinking about it again.

On average, a person has between 65,000 and 80,000 thoughts a day. Around 90% of those thoughts are the exact same thoughts as yesterday. The majority of the time you are awake is spent with automatic behaviours. So you're in a vicious cycle. It feels easier to live the cycle than try and change things. And who likes change? But you wouldn't stay in an abusive relationship, would you? And this is how *I* felt about alcohol.

I get it though, it's hard to stop that cycle. I've been there, and honestly, if you looked at me and my group of friends growing up and had to pick which one of us would end up tee total, I would most definitely be at the bottom of the list.

But here I am and I haven't had an alcoholic drink since 31st December 2018. Which currently stands at nearly eight hundred days. Please don't think I sit there counting the days. I have an app, as there is an app for everything these days. It also tells me that so far I have saved £4131.52! I can assure you that I have no idea where that money is, but I'm positive I would have found it each time I bought a bottle of wine and then money for the carb attack the next day.

It's not always been easy, and I want you to know that it is sometimes hard. Changing any habit initially requires willpower but then it takes so much more to continue. But what it has done is free up space in my head from all the thinking of should I or shouldn't I? I just don't – and space in my head is of a premium, believe me!

Even with a couple of years under my belt, I was still tempted, especially going into lockdown – and to be fair, it was quite stressful.

Looking on social media at everyone enjoying a beer or wine, having house parties for one, I'm not going to lie, it made me feel a bit jealous. Plus the boredom of not being able to go anywhere, I get it, what else is there to do?

But if I had decided to have a drink, it would still have been quite stressful, but with the added drawback of being hungover too and annoyed and ashamed at myself that I had failed.

Everyone was having online parties and Zoom party calls. It's hard enough on a Zoom call anyway to hear or not talk over each other, so these parties were just a rambling of screeches and laughing at nothing in particular. Even on a sober Zoom call it takes approximately 40-50 seconds to say goodbye and see who will press their screen first to leave the call – so with alcohol involved, it really is a ten minute affair to end a call.

But after, I felt the twinge of jealousy. I also got a massive wave of worry for people. A lot of people who don't normally drink in the house or don't drink on a 'school night' were getting into some really bad habits. Alcohol sales had risen by a third. One in five people admitted they were drinking more in this pandemic.

Drinking for me had a knock-on effect on everything else in my life. I never had one glass of wine, it one always lead to another, which led into staying up late, eating rubbish food, not washing my face or even cleaning my teeth when going to bed. This then resulted in a shit sleep, waking up at 3am thinking, 'God I feel rough. That's it, I'm not drinking tonight.' Getting through the day rather than enjoying the day. 7pm would come along and I'd think, 'OK, I'll just have one glass,' and repeat. By stopping that cycle, good habits just happened and I now have fresh breath going to bed. Result!

I don't want to come across preachy as this is just what is right for me. How do I know? Well, this is a small difference it has made in my life. Ted recently was singing a song he'd heard on TikTok (the bane of my life at the minute). The song was all about vodka. After he'd finished, I asked him "What is vodka?" He replied, "It's a drink the Russian mafia drink." This was such a relief as only a few years ago he was calling it "Mummy juice". Phew! Along with learning vodka songs on TikTok, Ted also makes me act out scenes where I have to mouth words in sync with someone else speaking. The bloody grief I get when I have done it wrong. He makes me do about twenty takes for one ten-second clip – a bloody perfectionist like his dad. Can you imagine doing that after a bottle of wine?

But at least I try. I recently learnt about a charity called NACOA, the National Association for Children of Addiction. I saw an interview about the services they offer. There is a helpline for children to ring, and I assumed they would just ring to chat about their parents being drunk. But I was wrong. Some rang for someone to read them a story at night as their parents were out of it; others rang to be able to tell someone, anyone, about getting a good result in their spelling test. It reminded me a bit of Childline, with Esther Rantzen appearing in adverts on TV, but more bespoke. I'm sure every person who is in their forties has tried to threaten their parents that they were phoning Esther but never got the reaction from their parents they'd expected. Having said that, after a bit of research, I see that Childline is still going strong and doing a lot of great work giving anyone under 19 someone to talk to on the phone for free.

Some of the children who called the NACOA helpline even did it with the knowledge of their parents and it suited them; it made it easier for them. This broke my heart. It made me think of the Stinks. I thankfully hadn't got to that stage, but how could someone not want to read their children a story at night? Don't get me wrong, part of me does understand. When Albie picks a really big book, I think "Bloody great, Albie, shall we not try this five-paged one instead?" But to not say goodnight and kiss your child, I just can't comprehend it.

Thinking back to kids I was in school with, I could guess now the ones that had that kind of life, and sadly, it doesn't really register until you're older. These situations then inevitably start the cycle and it goes on from there and follows on to their children.

A friend called Laura contacted me on social media. I'd met Laura a few years back when I had set up a business selling aloe vera. (I'm sure you know the one). I was convinced this business was going to change my life, so much so that Laura jumped on board too by becoming one of my team members. Laura was going to change her life too. We actually ended up changing our lives together, but not quite how we had imagined. She had seen I was sober and asked if I knew of any groups of like-minded people who meet up. I didn't but thought this was a great idea, so I asked Laura if she wanted to create one together.

We contacted a group called Bee Sober CIC and asked if we could become ambassadors for their group and create Bee Sober Bolton. They agreed and we set to organising.

Laura and I wanted events that scared you a little, take you out of your comfort zone, give you that adrenaline feeling. Due to lockdown, we were somewhat limited. We managed to arrange paddle boarding. I had never done this, but I was sure the hardest part would be putting on my wet suit over my lockdown body (remember, not your real body).

I forgot that my brain tumour the previous year had taken all my balance from my left side and this was only just improving. Small thing, but I suppose balance is quite integral to paddle boarding. We got on the boards and were given a paddle and told to crack on. That's about it really.

Initially we all sat down, but I said to myself: 'Irene, come on, be brave and stand up', so I did, fell straight in and nearly had a panic attack because of the cold. I actually couldn't breathe. Oh here we go again, physio for learning how to breathe again. (See book one – I forgot how to breathe.) The instructor asked if I was OK. I warbled, "Y Y Yes, I'm f f f fine." Paddle boarding – tick.

As I said previously, I believe I met Emma through fate. Another example of fate was one day at work. I was just reaching my one year target when I saw a poster at work highlighting alcohol awareness and the name of someone who was there if you'd like a chat.

This is when I met Mo. I'd seen Mo around the office, and she won't be offended by me saying this, but you can't help but notice her. Mo has a mass of black curly hair and bright red lips. Unlike the majority of people in our office.

I wanted to tell you both Mo's and Laura's stories, because personally I think they're amazing ladies and brave telling their stories. As you will read, they are both very different accounts.

MO'S STORY

Overcoming addiction

I grew up in inner city Manchester in the 70's. I had a good upbringing, didn't come from a drinking environment, so it wasn't learned behaviour. I was doing well at school. I was happy.

I started to work on the fairground at fifteen, for Saturdays/during school holidays. For those that know Manchester, it was at Belle Vue. I loved the atmosphere and the people there. I was a young, impressionable girl. The reward at the end of the day was a bottle of beer.

The first time I tasted this bottle of beer I was hooked. I didn't like the taste but I loved the feeling it gave me. There were lads working on the dodgems who would only drink half their bottles and I would finish off their drinks too.

Within weeks I was carrying drink around with me in my bag. I told my mother I didn't want to do my exams at school. Back then you had the option of leaving at fifteen, so I did.

I started to work full time at the fair. I had money now. I would buy a drink called Cherry B in a little bottle and carry around a bottle opener - all this at fifteen years old. Looking back at my life, I realise the alcohol had got me then. I suddenly felt more confident, I felt prettier.

After a few years, I left that job and got a job in an office. The thing I always looked forward to was going to the pub on a Friday.

I didn't like going anywhere unless there was a bar there. I didn't have relationships as such, I just went with the crowd to wherever the alcohol was.

I met the man I later married and got pregnant at nineteen. That was the only time I didn't drink. While I was pregnant with my son I stayed sober. The relationship with my husband was a toxic one. I was knocked unconscious when I was eight months pregnant by him and I still stayed there. I was very needy and codependant.

As soon as my son was born, when I was still in hospital, I said to my family, "Don't bring me flowers, bring me a couple of cans of Guinness."

When I left the maternity ward I went back to drinking as I had done previously, although it was now at a whole new level. I started a new job and found another drinker. As a drinker, you find and latch onto others with the same addiction. You seem to attract each other, so we latched on to each other. We would go drinking every day. I had cans of strong lager in my bag at work.

After fourteen years, I left my husband as he was getting in the way of my drinking. My son didn't want to come with me. My son stayed with my husband.

I ended up living in other people's houses; I had my matching luggage, which was two black bin bags. All I wanted to do was be somewhere, anywhere, were no one mithered me and I could just drink.

I took early retirement and got a lump sum from work and spent the next two years drinking that way.

It never occurred to me to cut down or stop. I began to lose blood. I was wearing a nappy because I had become incontinent and still it didn't occur to me.

I remember being sat on Market street in the city centre of Manchester with my bags, drinking a can of strong lager. I sat next to what I would call a bag lady. I turned to her and said, "I'm only drinking this cos it's a hot day and I don't want to queue up at McDonalds." She turned and looked at me and she knew exactly what I was. But still I couldn't see it.

My visits to my son had faded out.

I was forty-six and went to the doctor to tell her I thought I had an ulcer. I tried to stay away from the Doctors generally. She asked some questions and took some blood tests, which resulted in her telling me I had an alcoholic liver. I was angry and annoyed at her. She gave me a number for a support group.

I left the doctors, found a phone box and rang the number and I have never had an alcoholic drink since that day.

I am Mo and I am an alcoholic.
*read how Mo now helps others at the end of the book

LAURA'S STORY

Twelve months sober

Drinking for me, like for many others my age, pretty much came with part of being a teenager. I would save my dinner money each day at school for the weekend, where on a Friday and Saturday night I would buy three litres of cider, a packet of fags and sometimes have enough for a chip barm.

The habit I got myself into was binge drinking. As I got older I would drink more and more, drinking while getting ready, then pre drinks, then going out, then after parties. Nights would soon go and I'd still be drinking at 7am in someone's kitchen.

As the years passed by and adult life hit, babies and failed relationships, I found that I pretty much relied on drink for every situation. I didn't know who I was without alcohol. I never woke up and needed a drink, but I couldn't see a friend without making it into a heavy drinking session.

I would be the person who would avoid doing everyday things with friends, like trips to the cinema, just because that wouldn't include getting absolutely wasted. I was, I hate to admit, the person who called you 'boring' if you wasn't doing shots and rolling on the floor.

Drinking on nights out soon turned to also using drugs, mostly cocaine. The second I was out and had a drink, I couldn't get having some drugs off my mind. And the scary thing is that it really isn't that difficult to get your hands on some. You could pretty much ask most people in clubs if they could get some and you would be able to access it in 30 minutes.

My life became totally revolved around having a drink. I started to drink at home and it went from a bottle of wine on a Saturday to three or four bottles of wine on Thursday, Friday and Saturday.

Sometimes I would get cocaine at home if I had people round.

I would spend the week with overwhelming anxiety, so ashamed of my actions. I would have complete blackouts, arguments with my husband. Sometimes I wouldn't come home because I felt so down and hopeless. It was safe to say that I was severely depressed and just getting myself into a huge, huge hole. Somehow I would make excuses for myself: I didn't have a problem, 'I don't drink everyday', ' I don't wake up and need a drink'.

The reality is I DID have a problem with alcohol, it completely controlled me.

When I was young and I went out, I would laugh and dance with my friends. In the last few years of my drinking, I wasn't fun to be around. I was angry and sad and used going out to sit and speak to people about how I felt because I just wasn't honest with myself or others when I hadn't had a drink. I completely lost who I was, what I enjoyed, how to actually love myself and look after myself.

I made the decision to quit and I am now coming up to twelve months sober.

I'm sure the majority of you reading this will be able to have one glass of wine and that be it and that's great, but that's just not me. I'm an all or nothing kind of person with every aspect of my life. I'm sure some therapist could analyse me and tell me I'm not normal, but hey ho, who is? The people who I am meeting on my sober journey are similar to me. I bet if you hiked up Mount Kilimanjaro and chatted to the people up there, over half of them had given up something addictive. I wouldn't know though, as sadly my addiction hasn't transferred to hiking – or to be honest, any form of exercise, more to cakes!

With dieting, when I was younger and slimmer, I would eat a banana for breakfast, go all day without anything else, do two classes at the gym (as opposed to one) and go out and drink copious amounts of alcohol. Everything with me is either 0% effort or 110% effort. I can stick to any slimming program 100% for three weeks, lose nearly a stone because I hardly eat anything, then binge for the following three weeks.

It's like this book. If anyone asks me how to start writing I say, "Just try and do half an hour a day." Great advice, Irene – if I'd stick to it. I do nothing for a week then totally binge for twenty-four hours, typing away though the night, three cans of Red Bull to keep me awake. So basically, what I'm saying is, if any therapist out there needs a volunteer/model to test out new ways to fix someone like me, I am a willing guinea pig – free of charge obvs! I'll even do before and after photos. I'm not precious about sending them out to random people.

DIANE'S STORY

A little something extra in the lunchbox

I went on a night out, and because I'm tight, I decided to take my own vodka which I had bought previously from Krakow – vanilla flavour and very strong. I put the vodka into a blackcurrant Fruit Shoot bottle and tucked it into my handbag.

The next morning I checked my bag and found the Fruit Shoot bottle still full of vodka and for some reason put it back in the fridge to use at a later date.

Fast forward to the Monday morning when we woke up late and I was rushing to make Harry's packed lunch. I grabbed a Fruit Shoot from the fridge and shoved it into his school bag.

When Harry came home from school he said to me, "Mummy, that Fruit Shoot in my lunch is off! I put the bottle to my lips and it felt funny."

The horror began to set into my brain that I had sent my six-year-old to school with a bottle full of mega strong Polish vodka!

I asked Harry calmly if he had told Mrs Webster, the dinner lady. And thankfully he said, "No Mummy." Probably because he couldn't speak, due to either swollen lips or being unconscious...

The shame. It's funny now but it could have made Harry ill. In addition to social services knocking on my door.

JADE'S STORY

With ice and a slice

One day Rose and I were out walking; Rose was about three years old.

We stopped at a pedestrian crossing and waited for the green man alongside a lady.

The lady was chatting to Rose and went on to ask what Rose liked to drink, to which she replied, "I mostly like gin and tonics."

She went to add she liked it with ice and lime! The shame!

If you are sober curious, then now is the time to start doing a bit of research. Try reading someone else's story. There are so many books out there. Get in touch with me and I can tell you my favourites.

Why not, in your 'big' shop, try a couple of alcohol free or low alcohol versions. There are again lots out there and they are surprisingly good.

Although the majority of this chapter is about my habits with alcohol, it could relate to so many other things: food, exercise, self care, spending money, smoking, biting your nails, sucking your thumb at forty-five (again, this might be just a 'me' thing).

We all have habits. A lot of our habits are good and create a shortcut in the brain to behaving and feeling a certain way. If we had to really think about every single thing we did each day it would be exhausting, so our brain creates a shortcut. For example, I get up in a morning, wash my face, clean my teeth, then have a brew. I do all those things automatically. If I had to really think about each one, I'd be going back to my bed after having my brew because I'd be worn out.

So it's all about creating these shortcuts for good habits and trying to stop the shortcuts for the bad habits.

THREE THINGS I AM GRATEFUL FOR IN 2020:

• Staying alcohol free.

• Meeting Mo and Laura.

• Not sending my children into school with vodka.

SELF-HELP TIPS
Breaking bad habits

Your life is, to a large extent, is the sum of all your habits – good or bad.

Habits are a way for your brain to save energy, and we all approve of saving energy. So when you're driving to work you do it automatically, your subconscious part of your brain has saved this habit (creating a well-trodden path) and enabled you to do it without much thought.

When we were allowed out, I used to have a drink while I was getting ready, didn't think much about it as that's what I did and what my subconscious remembered me doing. It became an issue when I could finish a bottle before I had left the house.

You have to re-programme your subconscious mind to establish a new habit, so maybe getting ready for a night out entails dancing to music whilst getting ready rather than opening a bottle of wine.

Sounds simple. If only it was.

I am going to give you some tips that I used and still do to stop my bad/unhelpful habits – although I still suck my thumb, so nothing worked there!

1. Planning is key. Set out what you want to do and why you want to do it and don't veer off the track. The first few days/weeks you need to plan to the nth degree.

2. There will always be a reason or an occasion not to do it, so start today.

3. We all have a voice in our heads that tries to justify us breaking the rules and giving in to the habit. Ignore her, she's a witch!

4. Tackle one bad habit at a time.

5. Go to bed early. This helps with stopping bad habits like eating shite and drinking at night, but also you're creating a new good habit.

6. Read books on changing habits.

7. Join social media pages for the habit you want to quit. You don't even have to post or comment, you can be a lurker. But it just helps to know you are not alone.

8. Initially don't put temptation in front of you. You don't need bad food in the house, you don't need that bottle of vodka in the cupboard or packet of cigarettes in your secret drawer, chop your thumb off (for those thumb suckers – maybe too extreme?)

9. Pick a hobby that's new, a challenge. You could climb up Mount Kilimanjaro...or not.

10. Don't look at it as giving up something, look at it as what you will gain.

Mummy didn't NEED WINE, SHE NEEDED TO FIND HER TRUE SELF WITHOUT THE MASK OF ALCOHOL.

September

My car had finally arrived. My previous conversation with Adam about the car hadn't ended particularly well. I hadn't got round to telling him what make of car it was. How was I going to tell my 6'5" husband I'd bought a Mini – and not even one of the chunky fat ones, a teeny tiny mini!

His first journey in my car wasn't how I had imagined. He was unable to sit straight in the seat and his knees were up near his chin. It did make me laugh anyway as he glowered away.

Ah well, at least the Stinks fit in it, as schools were now open and I was able to drive them – wahoo!

This was the first time the Stinks would be putting on a uniform since March. The few weeks they had gone in before the holidays was like a holiday club – no uniforms and no lessons. I had prepared everything the night before. Their school trousers were a tiny bit snug. But we were all feeling that!

I wasn't sure how I should have been feeling inside. Should I feel anxious for them that they were going back to school when we didn't fully understand about Covid? Should I feel anxious for them that it was going to be a different experience than before and there would be new rules for them to remember on top of catching up on what they had missed? I didn't know what I *should* have been feeling, but what I did know was that I was feeling pretty effin' elated that I was getting my week days back. I waved them off at the gates and did a Dick Van Dyke kick in the air as I walked back to my teeny tiny car.

CAROL'S STORY
First day back

After sending Leo back to school, I went to collect him on his first day. I was anxious for him. Would he have settled back in OK? Was the work now too hard for him as he had missed so much?

I stood at the school gates and Leo came running out. I couldn't work out from his expression how the day had gone.

"Have you had a good day at school, Leo?" His reply was, "Have your boobies still got milk in them, Mummy?"

I don't know why I bothered worrying.

We had survived the lockdown of 2020 (I wasn't aware at this stage that there was going to be lockdown 2.0 and 3.0!) This survival I was going to use as the beginning of gaining some control over my life again.

I'm going to be completely honest with you now (not that I haven't been for the rest of this book, to be fair!). As you know, after I had Albie I was diagnosed with post-natal depression. I was also grieving for our son, Dusty. When I went to the doctors and cried uncontrollably in her office, telling her I thought Albie was going to die, she prescribed me some tablets and they helped.

Now for me, these were only ever meant to be a short-term solution. I took them for twelve months and I felt better – not happy all the time like Timmy Mallett from *Wacaday*, just balanced. I felt able to cope with day-to-day life, whereas before, small things had tipped me over the edge. I talk a lot about feeling like my head was going to implode and that's exactly how I felt without them.

On the other hand, I hated the feeling of being reliant on someone or something else (i.e. doctors/ tablets/ alcohol) to control how I was going to feel day to day. I felt ashamed and embarrassed that I was taking these in the first place, even though I was on the lowest dose. Even now, why do I feel the need to try and justify the fact that they were a low dose? But I do. I needed help at the time and I got it through with medication and it worked.

I'm ashamed to say I never really bought into depression and anxiety before having post-natal depression and used to think people should just pull themselves together. I thought people who committed suicide were being selfish. But now I understand more (not everything) about mental health and wellbeing and I know that they honestly thought what they did was the right thing for everybody around them. It is heart-breaking for someone to think the world would be a better place without them in it.

I understand now that telling someone who is depressed to pull themselves together is much like saying to someone with a broken leg to just walk it off. It's not how it works.

In 2018 I had decided I was going to come off the tablets and then I was diagnosed with Brian the brain tumour, so I convinced myself then was not the right time. But like giving up alcohol, when was there ever going to be a right time? I'm a big believer in focusing on one thing at a time, as I've tried the whole 'cut down on alcohol, diet, exercise and learn new things' all at the same time, but this is where I've failed in the past. If I succumb to one of those, then in my head I rationalise that I may as well succumb to all the rest and be done with it.

So after Brian was removed and I had learnt more about self-help, I knew it was now or never. I now had the tools to do it. The tablets had always felt like a safety net, so I never threw them out or anything rash like that, but I wanted to see if the skills I had learnt over the past few years could enable me to go at life without them.

Brian had gone, I had stopped drinking (we all know this adds to anxiety), I meditated every night, I still ate shite, but hey, we can't all be perfect. We had gotten through lockdown and now, more than ever, I felt ready to do it.

I needed to start slowly; you can't just stop taking a medication like this. I didn't tell anyone I had made the decision, very much like when I gave up alcohol. I didn't need the added pressure of anyone else knowing. And as very few people knew about me taking the medication in the first place, that was quite easy.

I started taking one every other day. Initially, I didn't feel any different so I got a bit trigger happy and stopped for a full two weeks – cue total meltdown at something so insignificant that I can't remember what it was. I went back on them, but I knew it was only to get me ready to try again.

Trying again, I went with one tablet every other day for a month. I decided to reach out to the friends that did know about the medication and let them know what I was attempting and how I was feeling.

My friendship group is varied and I have different topics of conversations with each of them. I talk to one invariably about diets, food and my lack of willpower, another about kids, one who I run by all my wacky business ideas, another moaning about husbands. I have a couple of friends who encompass all those categories and these are my closest friends. Ones I can literally tell anything to and I know they wouldn't judge me. They might say, "Actually Irene, I think you're being a knob," but I can take things like that from these friends without being offended – most of the time.

HOLLY'S STORY
Don't you just love kids

I work in a school, and as we all know, children say the funniest things.

One day, the teacher asked if the children could point shapes out in the playground - circles, squares - which they did. Then one child said, "What about a semi-circle?"

Another child said, "Yes, I can see two semi-circles, the bags under your eyes."

The teacher had no response.

Don't you just love kids!

We all need that friend with who we can get out all our nastiness. Like a counsellor for your bad thoughts, unload them all and then be kind again. It is good to be kind, but it's sometimes tricky. I think that it is good for our mental wellbeing to get all the nastiness out, as it can eat you up inside when you see someone wearing a hideous outfit and you can't tell anyone. Like the women you see in Tesco with her Primarni leggings on and you can see the pattern of her knickers through them. You need an outlet for this kind of stuff. Or is this just me?

Plus there are different forms of communication with each friend: the friend you only communicate though voice notes, the one you only use WhatsApp with, the very few that you have an actual phone call with, the friends you send a text message to and they immediately ring you back (if I had wanted a chat, I would have rung in the first place), and the friend that always ring you at the most inappropriate times (generally the one who hasn't got kids and rings at 7.30pm while you are chasing a Stink around the house with a pair of pyjamas in your hand saying "5,4,3,2,1" for the umpteenth time.)

I'm a big message sender and it is often my preferred form of contact. (Unless you are one of my friends that I complain about Adam to, which is done via voice notes or telephone call because I'm usually that angry my fingers won't work properly to text. Obviously, this happens very rarely, Adam!) As you probably know by now, I usually rush things or get distracted easily. So I make mistakes or send a message to someone completely random and then don't understand why I've not had any replies.

MY FAMILY'S TOP FIVE MESSAGE BLUNDERS:

5 My sister Catherine was in the car and having a row with her then boyfriend, Sean. Sean got out of the car and went into a shop. Catherine quickly messaged her friend saying "Sean is a knob." Sean came out of the shop with a face like thunder after receiving his message from Catherine.

4 My sister Hannah once emailed the Dean of the University where she was working and signed it off 'Hannah Laycock'. Just as she pressed send, predictive text altered it to 'Banana Laycock'.

3 I was sent an email in work and there was a full thread of other conversations attached. Being nosey, I read though them all and then decided to forward it to my boss, explaining that I thought the two people chatting on the email were no doubt having an affair. Instead of forward, I pressed 'reply to all', including the two people I was gossiping about.

2 Hannah posted on social media that she was now a born again vegan, although Facebook had other ideas and changed the word 'vegan' to 'virgin'.

And in at number 1...

1 My biggest fuck up was when I was on a girls holiday and I sent my sisters a message saying how good the holiday was and I had copped off (it was the nineties) three times already...only to send it to my boyfriend at the time. Strangely, he never replied...ever again!

I now message people before I ring. Or diary in a call… When did that start happening? When did life become so busy that even a telephone call had to be diarised? What did we do before mobile phones were invented and you just had to take your life into your own hands by answering the phone having no idea who was on the other end? Talk about living dangerously.

When I was around eleven years old, I picked up the landline phone: "399674 Hello." A man started to talk and asked me my name. Being young and naïve, I told him. He then asked, "What colour knickers do you have on, Irene?" I was shocked. I put the phone down and it rang straight away again. I turned to Catherine and said, "Will you get that?" Catherine was seven – I was a great big sister. I heard Catherine say, "No, it's Catherine." Then her mouth dropped open and her eyes nearly popped out of her head. "Put the phone down, Catherine, put it down." We ran upstairs and hid. Oh, those were the days; it's not like that anymore with the internet. The perverts haven't got that personal touch anymore.

We were once flashed at as well. That was common practice amongst perverts back in the day. I wonder where they have all gone now? To the dark, dark web I'm guessing. But for a flasher, does it have the same satisfaction as seeing someone's face in shock when they showed someone their flaccid knob.

KERRY'S STORY
My mum Florence (76 yrs)

My mum gets confused quite easily with lots of things and many times we roll around laughing at the text messages she sends - usually half in lower case and the rest in capitals.

She rang me one morning to tell me what had happened overnight on her street.

She said, "Oh Kerry, you won't believe what happened last night. A man on the street had his windows all smashed in and his car trashed with bricks. It was madness!"

My reply: "My God, Mum, are you OK? Why would someone do that?"

My mum: "I don't know but the man that lives there is called Pedro, they wrote it on his wall."

I was thinking, 'Oh my God, what is the world coming to when someone from another country cannot feel safe in his own home?'

I visited my mum later that day as I was concerned about what had gone on the night before and to see Pedro's house. The letters P A E D O were written on the wall.

God love my mum!

Back to my tablets: after the initial month of taking them every other day, I started to forget to take the odd tablet and never even noticed. There wasn't this big epiphany. It just slowly happened that I took less and less and felt exactly the same. I was expecting some big waves of lows in my life, but that didn't happen, so maybe the tools I had learnt were the ones I needed after all.

To keep me grounded, I was focused on my goal of my book being made into a TV series. The Stinks were thankfully back at school and took all the changes in their stride. It was now normal for them to have their temperature taken and wash their hands every five minutes. They now had their lunches in their bubbles and stayed with their bubbles throughout the day. Kids are so resilient. I wonder what age we become sensitive to change?

We all felt so much better getting our routines back. People started looking forward to things again, smiling and saying hello as you passed them in the street rather than hiding behind our masks.

During this month, I was informed I had been nominated for two awards: HER-abilities award (which is for women who have overcome challenges in their life and turned them around) and a lifetime achievement award in a local Health and Wellbeing event. The only awards I have ever won, as I said previously, were most improved player in our street's rounders team – and I shared that award with a nine year old who, in all honestly, probably deserved it more than I did – and a medal for twenty years police service (and to be fair, that just celebrated the fact that I had turned up for work for the past twenty years.) However, I was very proud of those awards and who doesn't love a medal! The Stinks think it's amazing.

I was a bit perplexed at the lifetime achievement as I was still only forty-four years old and I wasn't quite sure what I had achieved more than the average person, but hey, I wasn't knocking them back.

A couple of weeks later, I received an email saying that because there wasn't an abundance of people nominated for the HER-abilities women award, by default, I was now in the finals. Wahoo! That sums up my life to a tee! Getting there, but by default. I wasn't complaining.

These finals could be a practice run for my BAFTA award. I must remember to write my acceptance speech when I get a minute. We don't want another Gwyneth Paltrow moment.

THREE THINGS I AM GRATEFUL FOR IN 2020:

• Speaking out when I needed help.

• Deciding I no longer needed that help.

• Getting my BAFTA award speech ready.

SELF-HELP TIP

There is no shame in seeking help.

I just want to reiterate here that this is just my experience with anti-depressants. Everyone is different and I am by no way an expert. As everyone's story is different, I don't feel qualified to speak about anything other than my experience here. There are plenty of experts out there who specialise in these things. If you are on medication, please don't just stop taking them, it needs to be done on the advice of your doctor.

Reach out to friends and family too. But I get it, sometimes it's easier to speak to a stranger as you know that what you said when you were at your lowest will not be thrown back in your face over Christmas dinner three years later.

I do wish I had not taken the medication in the first place and instead looked at different techniques and used medication as a last resort, but at the time I didn't have the energy or the inclination to do this.

The medication did help as a stop gap until I did have the energy to research other techniques, just a longer stop gap than I would have liked.

But once I had taken the decision to stop, I realised that I could have done it a long time ago. I think many of us underestimate how strong we really are. We're effin' superwomen, don't you know. We can handle anything.

Don't look Back
My Darling,
YOU'RE NOT
GOING THAT WAY.

October

Making a TV program takes time, and as we've already established, I lack somewhat in the patience department. But as this was my ultimate dream, I was prepared to *try* and be patient at least. I refrained from ringing every day just to check where we were up to. Play it cool, Irene, play it cool.

Then one week I received an email: 'Could we diarise in a call for later in the week?' My gut feeling was this wasn't good news. I tried to keep visualising my BAFTA awards night but it felt like it was slipping away. While I was visualising receiving my award and air kissing Adam, menial tasks started to get in the way, like washing school uniforms, shopping lists, wiping arses…no Irene, concentrate.

On speaking to the TV company, I was told that due to outside issues, the company couldn't take my project on although they truly believed in it. They wished me luck for the future. Devastated doesn't quite cut it. I felt like I had been unceremoniously dumped by a boyfriend. I just didn't see it coming. I tried to be the total professional on the phone but then started to cry. Bloody hell, Irene, that's not very professional, is it?

I have only ever been dumped by someone once before, which I didn't see coming either. He said I was high maintenance. How rude! I don't think it was said in a way that I like to look on point at all times and won't go anywhere without nails, hair, makeup, Botox done – as you're aware, I'm shite at girly things. I don't think he liked the fact that each morning he could wake up and get a different Irene. Wow, some people are so picky.

I suppose the fact that I was in talks in the first place was an achievement in itself and there were worse things going on in the world, but I allowed myself to wallow in some self-pity for a few days, eating cake and chocolate. Strangely, alcohol never came into my mind – another achievement right there.

After I had wallowed, I wrote to the TV company and apologised for crying on the phone. I decided to pull my big girl pants up (which were definitely getting bigger as the year went on) and move forward.

I had stopped writing when I thought I was going to be a TV star and had focused on things that would work well on television. So out this book came again and I got stuck in.

I'm not going to take the picture of my BAFTA award off my vision board, as now I'd had a glimpse of what could be, my goals remained the same. I was just going to have to work harder or smarter…or both.

After my week of self-pity, I decided to write down everything that was out of my control in that moment and then throw that shit away. I then wrote things that were under my control and started to work on them.

THINGS UNDER MY CONTROL	THROW THAT SHIT AWAY THINGS
The amount of shite I consume daily	COVID
The amount of money I spend on Amazon	Other people's decisions
The amount of time I spend on social media	When the bin men don't turn up on a Tuesday

There was no point in dwelling on things. We had lots of nice things to focus on and Albie's impending 6th birthday was one of them.

I did what I do best. I created a Pinterest board for birthday theme ideas. I know the Stinks are only eight and six, but I think I've already peaked with birthday party planning. We have had superhero training parties, scientist experiment parties, and bowling parties (where Ted wore a box on his head the whole time).

God knows what I'm going to plan for their 21st birthdays. I will have run out of ideas by then so it will probably end up being a trip to McDonalds and a McFlurry for a treat.

EMMA'S STORY
Mmmmm tasty!

At Jude's 4th birthday party, he had decided on a Batman theme. We spent a small fortune on the best Batman cake we could find, which he loved.

All his friends arrived and one of his friends was equally in awe of the Batman cake and as soon as he saw it he licked it all over! Pre Covid, but still!

FAYE'S STORY
A grand entrance

At my niece's birthday party, I had the job of carrying the immense birthday cake in whilst all the children sang Happy Birthday.

I was so careful walking. I could not drop this cake. All thirty children had their eyes on me as I slowly brought the cake in.

As I walked into the room, my tights fell down. Not just a little bit, they literally fell to my ankles. All I could do was keeping walking and singing.

The Stinks had settled back into their new routines at school with no problems. Kids are ace, so resilient. One afternoon I collected Albie. His face was red and his hair was a sweaty mess. Initially I thought 'Bloody hell, he's had a hard day.' Then he immediately started crying on seeing me, telling me he missed everyone. Albie is not one for gushing emotion so I knew then that something wasn't right. As soon as we got home I checked his temperature. Thankfully, a thermometer was one of the 'things in demand' that we had been able to acquire early on. He slept as soon as he got home – again not normal for Albie.

Oh no, he had Covid! Cue being on the phone for the rest of the evening, whilst simultaneously pressing refresh on the NHS Covid test site, trying to locate a Covid test which wasn't at the other end of the country.

It was ridiculous. I was willing to drive some distance but couldn't get one anywhere. I heard from colleagues that we could get a test through work and all we had to do was just send a quick email.

I sent the email at 7am. As I was sending the email, Ted woke up coughing. Oh dear God, they both had it!

I received an email back saying that we were allowed one test per family and we had to be at the test centre at midday that day. The next few conversations between Adam and I were discussing which child was our favourite to get the test done. We decided to do a list. Their pro and cons.

TED		ALBIE	
The oldest	+5	Albie was still in the cute phase	+10
Ted was in the bad attitude stage	-10	It was nearly Albie's birthday (part of his birthday present?)	+5
Ted had a cough	+5	Albie had a high temperature	+5
Ted has good hair	+5	Albie had a mop head	-5

After much discussion, we decided our favourite was Albie. Ted was going through a little shite stage, so yes Albie was our favourite at this precise moment in time. Only kidding Ted…or am I?

On driving into the test centre, it was desolate. There was a big sign as we drove in saying 'Do not open your windows'. We were directed to a hut where a lady came out and held up messages on cards. It felt quite surreal, like a zombie apocalypse film. I was told to open my window a small amount and face the other way. I know Covid is serious but this started the inappropriate giggles. She threw the test through the small gap in the window and threw me a dirty look whilst she was at it. Of course I couldn't resist turning my head to see what she was doing. We were directed to drive on.

On parking up, I read all the instructions as Albie sat on my knee. Can I just say at this stage that both Stinks had miraculously got better and were laughing and climbing all over the car. I shouted, "Please can you at least look ill!"

I gave the test to Adam and said, "You read the instructions and I'll do the test." But I think all Adam heard was, "Blah blah blah." Adam handed me the swab and said, "Put that up his nose as far as you can reach", which I did. It wasn't pleasant for Albie or me. I finished that one and Adam gave me the container to place the swab in. I broke off the end and sealed the container. I then asked Adam for the second swab for Albie's throat. He showed me the bag and it was empty. No more swabs. *I* then read the instructions and it stated to use the same swab for both the nose and the throat. We had to then put our hazard lights on the car to alert a Covid volunteer to come with another test. Explaining what I had done through a closed window. Again, we faced the other way while she threw the test through the window. And so we started again. I re-did the test, much to Albie's delight, Ted watching on from the back seat, thanking God he wasn't the favourite child today. Finally, we completed the test after making Albie gag, which in turn made me gag. What is that all about? It's like the yawning thing. If I see someone gag it makes me gag.

I'm hoping at least this experience will put them off faking it for a while.

We drove on as directed and gave the completed test to a man at a Portakabin who explained that we would receive the results within twenty-four hours. Although I could have predicted the results myself by this stage.

The text came back negative – which was no surprise after his miracle recovery at the test centre. We could now concentrate on his birthday plans. At last, a bit of normality.

KATE'S STORY

Catching up with old colleagues

Gareth, my husband, was on a late shift and I went in to give my daughter Molly a kiss before I went to bed. She sat up and projectile vomited in my face, hair, all over my PJ's, etc. and then started choking. I ended up with her over my knee, slapping her back, but she was really struggling and turning a strange shade, so I rang 999.

The ambulance arrived really quickly and we were whisked to A&E, where we were treated fantastically and Moll bounced back after being admitted for the night.

In my haste, I had forgotten to take my phone with me and the staff said I could use the landline on their desk to ring Gareth and get him to bring fresh clothes, etc. As I was doing this, I turned to see two of my old colleagues (who I used to party with regularly before I settled down). The look on their faces when they realised the PJ-clad, vomit-soaked woman was me was an absolute picture. Never mind my dignity...at least Moll was OK.

Four days before Albie's birthday, Boris introduced a tier system, and just our luck, we were in tier three, meaning there would be no party for Albie after all.

The tier three rules were: no mixing with another household, no hospitality open, no entertainment venues open, no restaurants open and no travelling to other areas unless it is for work or education. So fundamentally, acting as though you're in a lockdown but we'll now call it tier three.

We decided we had to do something special, so we went to a park for the day in our little bubble. The Stinks had a great day. I tried to go on all the equipment with them rather than sit and watch them. Taking them to the park is usually to give me a break. I once saw a meme about a women frowning at another mother using her mobile phone whilst her kids were on the park. It said 'How do you know the mum on her phone is not researching healthy meals to serve to her kids, or researching educational activities?' But why should it be that? I'm usually scrolling through Facebook checking out the gossip and having a break from my kids, which I think is acceptable.

KAREN'S STORY
I'll be five minutes

We decided to have a short break in Conway, Wales. It's our favourite family destination.

One day, we all went down to the harbour on a lovely, bright, sunny day.

After lots of walking, we decided to have a rest by the harbour and chill for a couple of hours. We found a lovely spot and I pulled out my camp chair and settled down to read a book. Bill decided he was going to a beer tent nearby to buy a drink. Meganne and Katie, nine and six years old, asked if they could go to explore, which I agreed to.

Around twenty minutes later, Bill returned with his beer and asked where the girls were. I explained they were off having an adventure. Bill looked out across the harbour and eventually saw the girls stuck up to their knees in sludge. There had been there the whole time, stuck, and had been trying to get my attention.

Bill ran to rescue them and pull them out of the sludge. By now, a small crowd had gathered and had seen what was happening. They watched Bill struggle in the mud, trying to rescue the girls and salvage their wellington boots.

Bill is usually a very laid-back man, but on this day he was blazing. He brought the girls, covered in mud, back to me and said, "You've made a show of us, over to you." I had to take the girls to the nearest toilets and clean them up using paper toilet roll and water.

The day after, we had all calmed down and headed off to the Great Orme, Llandudno. At the time, I was scared of heights so I stayed at the bottom reading and waiting for Bill and the girls to return from their adventure.

Whilst there, Bill took Katie and Meganne to the park. They were playing happily when he told them, "I'm just going to the toilet. I'll be five minues. Do not go anywhere."

When Bill returned, they were nowhere to be seen.

They had forgotten what Bill had said and gone looking for him. They wandered into a nearby café and explained that they had lost their daddy. The kind café owner asked them what their dad looked like. They explained he was tall with a big red bald head.

Bill was frantic looking for the girls and searched high and low. He ran into the café. On seeing Bill, the café owner exclaimed, "Ah, here he is!"

Obviously the 'tall with a big red bald head' was a perfect description! He swore the girls to secrecy and I have only recently been told this.

So all in all, an eventful holiday.

Back to our birthday day out in the park. I went on everything apart from the swings or roundabouts. I can't do those, they make me feel seasick. I even get seasick on a lilo. Around two o'clock I felt very dodgy. I'd stayed away from the seasick-inducing equipment, so I knew it wasn't that. I would liken it to a major hangover but without the bender the night before. I told Adam he was going to have to take over and I went back to the car, where I spent the rest of the afternoon asleep. I never sleep anywhere other than my bed (these days anyway). I'm one of those that needs my pyjama's on and to be in bed before I can even attempt a sleep, so I knew I wasn't well. Oh no, I had spent the morning walking around a bloody park!

That night I wanted chicken soup – again, another indicator at how ill I was. When I was ill as a child, my mum always made homemade chicken soup. She did it for us all. She has been known to still make it and drop it off even when we had our own houses. Myself and Adam sat eating the soup and I asked him, "Can you actually taste this soup?" to which he replied, "No, although I thought it was just your cooking." He said 'cooking', but we both knew he meant 'opened the tin of Heinz and put it in the pan.' It goes without saying.

The next day, we both managed to get tested and within hours the results came back positive. Effin' great!!! Now we had to isolate with two Stinks (who thankfully didn't have any symptoms, but unfortunately had an abundance of energy) and two sick parents, and we couldn't leave the house for two weeks – fourteen effin' days!

Luckily, family and friends rallied round and left food on the doorstep. I spent a lot of time in bed sleeping through it. Adam wasn't as poorly as me so I thought he could sit downstairs with the Stinks. One day, after being asleep for about three hours, I turned over in bed to find Adam fast asleep in bed next to me. I've no idea how long the Stinks were fending for themselves, but they lived.

Adam and I recovered after a few weeks. Our sense of taste didn't come back straight away so I was able to convince Adam each meal I served tasted fantastic and it was just a shame his taste buds were missing out.

Back to regaining some normality. So back to writing, seeing as though Michelle Keegan and Jason Statham weren't going to be hearing from me anytime soon.

THINGS I AM GRATEFUL FOR IN 2020:

• I nearly had a TV show.

• The Stinks didn't have Covid.

• Adam and I survived (our two weeks in isolation with the Stinks).

SELF-HELP TIP

Journaling, diary writing, doodling, whatever you want to call it

When you think of someone writing a diary, you think of a fourteen-year-old girl listing her top ten boys. But why is this another of those things that has to stop when you become an adult? I still write my top ten boys, but sadly Adam rarely makes the list. (Just kidding, Adam!)

I talk so much about writing being my therapy. I love journals, planners, notepads, lists, anything to free my mind up a little bit. For me, it offloads everything in my mind and then I feel in a better position to sort through it. I even write down the things I can't control and I then just throw that away. There's no point in spending time on negative things like that.

You can write anything that pops into your head. Some people also do this through drawing pictures - take Vincent Van Gogh for example, looking at his paintings, his head was proper f*@ked. Although he is probably not the best example to use as it didn't really do him much good.

I prefer writing myself. Journaling has been shown to improve your mood. It helps you prioritise problems and concerns. It's also a way to get to know yourself better. Know yourself, girl! (sorry, flashback from *Big Brother 2006*)

When are you ever really alone with your thoughts? It doesn't have to make sense or be grammatically correct, there is only you that will see it – unless you decide to stick it all in a book and publish it!

It is recommended that you write for fifteen minutes a day. There is a technique that people have started to do where you write three pages of words every morning. You do not let your pen leave the paper until you have completed it. A lot will be just random shite but you may write something that really resonates with you.

You know me well enough by now to know that I'm not going to be all rules – DO WHAT'S RIGHT FOR YOU.

There is
No Failure
– YOU EITHER WIN
OR LEARN.

November

November is always a hard month in our family. The first reason being most of my immediate family have their birthdays this month and the other reason is it is Dusty's birthday.

November is also the start of a routine of when the Stinks ask for anything, I suggest they stick it on their Christmas list. "You need a new pillow, Ted? Get it on your Christmas list." It's amazing how much Father Christmas can source these days, from toothpaste to new school uniforms.

Some extreme things the Stinks have asked for are a Lamborghini and five dogs. (not just the one then?) Now after learning from past experience, I sit with them and gently coax them into writing things that I have already bought and hidden somewhere (just not sure where). Once the letter is posted, there is no turning back. On Christmas Eve they usually come up with a random gift that will absolutely ruin their lives FOREVER if they don't get it on Christmas day.

We were still in tier three of lockdown, so other than school, work and a walk, there was very little we could do.

I continued writing my thoughts. I tried to concentrate on where I wanted to go. I wanted to gain back control of my dreams, and just because it didn't happen this time, it didn't mean to say it wouldn't happen in the future. It wasn't even on my radar twelve months previously. I'm not going to stop looking for

BAFTA dresses or tweaking my speech. I was going to try and take the positives from it and move on.

I do suffer from Imposter Syndrome – who doesn't from time to time? I think I get it worse when I actually put myself out there. I have even asked people for reviews; obviously, I'm only asking for good ones or constructive reviews, but even constructive ones I don't take too well. But there's always going to be the haters, the trolls, and I guess that comes with the territory.

Why is it that you receive numerous good comments but the one thing you focus on is the one negative comment? I decided to pay for a session on self-belief. Just speaking to someone that looks like they have got their shit together and talking through things can be enlightening. I talked about the doubts I had in my ability in writing and if I was going to be found out as being a fraud. But what I realised is how could I be a fraud when all I'm writing about is what's in my head. No one can dispute what is in my head.

Whilst in this self-belief session, I spoke about when I was a fresh-faced police officer with shiny boots. On one shift, I completed a report and my sergeant called me into his office. He had gone through my report with a red pen, crossing out sentences and writing how he felt it should be written. I felt like I was back at school and that knocked my confidence massively. After that, any report I wrote I asked at least one other person to read over it. I think subconsciously every time I wrote, I assumed someone would get a red pen out and scribble all over it.

Another topic we chatted about was about me wanting to run. I have always wanted to be a runner. Runners always look free to me; you don't need anything other than a pair of trainers and you can just run anywhere. I convinced myself I didn't have a runner's body – another comment from an old police boss about my boobs being too big to be a runner. There's a bit of a theme here. Why did these two events still have some control over my life twenty years on? I know serious athletes don't tend to have big boobs, but all I wanted was to jog five kilometres, and I'm sure there are runners out there with bigger boobs than me. Realistically, if I ever tripped up, surely the bigger boobs would be better. And anyway, if I took up running, it would be another opportunity for an online shopping spree of sports bras and new trainers.

So for the umpteenth time, I downloaded the Couch to 5K app. Well, as I'm all or nothing, I actually downloaded the Couch to 10K app – go big or go home. I can proudly say that I now run three times a week, wearing a sports bra that cuts off the circulation around my torso. I've not had any black eyes. I've not gotten to the feeling free stage yet, but I'm doing it and have passed week three! (Week three was always a quitting point for me.) This time it was different.

I announced it on social media, which made me feel like I couldn't quit. And although I'm still not at the loving it stage, the days when I run I feel amazing… afterwards. If I cancel on a run, I feel bad and often regret cancelling, so hopefully it is now a good habit that I have developed.

HELEN'S STORY
When you gotta go...

Back when I was training for the Ultra (50k run!), Scott, my running coach, and I had to complete our own marathon course as a training day. So off we set, bearing in mind it's January in Sydney so hot AF. We get about 6km in and all of a sudden I am busting for a pee. I tell Scott and he says, "OK, there's a service station in a few km, can you hold on?" I'm not too bad so I say yes. It's really common for runners to need to pee or poo but I'm not one of them. I think the adrenalin puts my poo right off.

But as I continue, the desire to pee is getting really strong, and since having Mia... (although Mia is now eleven!) Anyway, I need to pee real bad. I'm in a suburban street and I am weighing up post boxes (people's personal ones), garden walls, cars, etc. as potential sites where I can just pee behind. I'm really struggling. I can't talk, think, run. I just have an overwhelming desire to pee.

Scott encourages me on and we finally make it to the services. I'm in a world of pain and Scott has to go inside to get the key as the toilet is on the outer wall facing a main road. He gets the key and lets me in. I push him flying out of the way, slam the door shut, pull my shorts down and sit down. The relief is amazing.

As I am sitting there doing those exquisite wee shivers, I get another feeling, the back door feeling. The toilet is horrific (think Moor lane bus station at 3am on a Sunday morning condition), but I'm already sitting down so I think what the heck, I'm going to be messy after 42km anyway, so I go for it. My bowels just melt out of me. I must have dropped about 5kg and I am completely empty, but it's disgusting and the smell....anyway, I sort myself out, wash my hands and open the door and Scott is stood literally right there with two lorry drivers waiting behind him.

What did he hear? What can he smell? I'm horrified! I just tell him quietly that I did a poo too. He's like 'good for you, I may as well do a pee while I'm here' so just pushes passed me into my smell. I could've died. I then had about another 32km run of shame with me apologising for the state I left the toilet for him.

We still laugh about it now. Having said that, Scott always makes sure he goes in the cubicle first.

Now Ted had seen me back running (or attempting to run), he decided he wanted to restart football lessons. I know I shouldn't label my children at such a young age, but in our house, Albie is the one that excels at anything sporty and Ted is the more creative one. Although we have continued to try and find a sport that Ted enjoys, but we are running out of options.

I was pleased that he wanted to give it another go. As we always say in our house: just because you're not the best, it doesn't mean you should quit. (catchy, huh?) I know it's not the strongest of family mottos, but we seem to be saying it a lot in this house. I'm only learning this in my forties, so hopefully Ted will have a headstart on me. We booked them both in for a full day football training to see how they got on.

Later that day I went to collect them. Albie was full of beans, running out to the car to show me his award. Best player – aw, I was so proud. I could see Ted in the corner of my eye with a face like thunder. "How did it go, Ted?" "I hated it and Albie got an award so I boo'd him."

Albie went on to explain that as each child got an award, everyone (including Ted) clapped and cheered, but when Albie was receiving his, Ted boo'd him. I bet the instructors thought he was a right little shit. To be fair, they would have been right on this occasion.

We tried a day at tennis club. This wasn't a sport either had attempted yet so maybe it could be Ted's thing. I collected them at 3pm. Again, Albie was waving a certificate at me and Ted couldn't look me in the eye. I know that feeling, when all you want to do was cry and you are trying so hard to keep the tears back. Then seeing someone that loves you and you know if you make eye contact the tears will come streaming out. I still do it now with my mum.

I congratulated Albie swiftly and told Ted to sit in the front seat. As soon as we sat in the car, there was floods of tears – mine too. I hate seeing him like this and I just wanted to make it all OK for him. Albie shoved his certificate into Ted's face and said, "Here Ted, you can have it." This made me melt more. Here was Albie, not particularly arsed that he was awarded player of the day, and Ted would have killed for this certificate. Ted was fuming. If I'd have let him, it would have started with a sly dig in Albie's ribs, then Albie would have retaliated. Then we would have been at full-on scrap mode.

We have decided that for future sport days we are going to send them to different events and then the competition is healthy and doesn't carry on when they get home, developing into a full-on fight to the death.

Dusty's birthday was getting closer. He would have been seven this year. It's strange as the years go on, as you look at it differently. Sometimes I cry, but I try to see it as Dusty knew it just wasn't his time and he stepped back in order for Albie to arrive. I like this way of thinking. Some years I've planned to do things on his birthday, others I just let it pass by with just a thought and a walk to where his ashes are scattered.

This was last year's 8th November:

I wake up, lean over and kiss Adam, and say Happy Birthday to Dusty. We have a cuddle then I hear the screams from the Stinks having an enormous fight.

I go downstairs and spilt them up before making them eat breakfast from opposite sides of the lounge, not looking at each other. I then go on to find undies, socks and uniforms. They are in aged 8 and aged 6 clothes, so often in a morning they go off with each other's undies and uniforms on. This morning was no different as Ted's undies did seems bit snug!

Once dressed, they continue to fight and in my morning stress I shout, "I can't believe you are fighting on baby Dusty's birthday." Ted: "Sorry Mummy." Albie: "No, it's not his birthday." I think the lack of balloons and party poppers confused him. Dusty would have been six and I'm under no illusions that he wouldn't be stuck in, fighting too.

Then I feel guilty for what I've said, as they can't understand. So, I (try) give them extra cuddles, whilst Albie tries to pull away, and I beat myself up further about being a bad mum.

In the car, all set, I feel alright. I'm OK today, I think, no tears. My best friend phones me but I miss her call. I ring her back as I know she is ringing to ask if I'm OK. I get her answering machine, so I proceed to tell how I am fine and then start crying, blubbering into her answer machine, telling her how well I'm doing.

I pull myself together and remember I have a nice day planned out for myself. I have booked the day off work and am going to do nice things today.

Starting with a network event. It's at a local hotel near me and I walk into the main entrance. I don't ask the receptionist where I should be going and instead walk with a purpose, having no idea where to go and end up walking around and around the hotel trying to find the event. I'm terrible with reading the details, like the location of said events. When I eventually get there, I have a lovely morning talking to new people and make some good connections – I think.

I leave to go out for lunch with a friend, and on pulling out of the car park, drive straight into a metal barrier. Really!!! I only had the damage fixed last month where the last barrier attacked my car. Well this damage is going to have to stay till after Christmas as there are no spare pennies. So I just won't wash my car for the next couple of months – like I need an excuse.

Lunch is delicious, although I eat too much and then remember I have booked myself in for a full body massage at 2pm where I am going to have to lie on my belly which is now nicely rounded and full of food.

At the massage place I drink a load of water to try and diffuse my food baby. My massage is lovely, although the relaxing music keeps stopping, which is slightly distracting, but hey, it was a Groupon offer so can't complain too much. (Forever the tight arse.)

As the lady reaches my feet, I remember I have three-week-old red nail polish on about six nails. Which now I'm really embarrassed about, but I'm sure she's seen worse.

I get dressed, semi relaxed, and feel very muggy – must be the oils. On arriving home, I realise I have caught Adam's bug. The bug that he has been complaining about for the past week and I have just ignored – even muttering the words 'he is a wimp'.

I'm supposed to be going watching Adam DJing in a club, and the Stinks are having a sleepover at my mum's. He starts his set at 10pm and it ends at 3.30am. I am usually in bed at 9pm and asleep at 10pm, so the thought of it isn't too appealing in the first place.

I make some excuse to Adam (don't want him thinking I'm a wimp too) and get in my pj's, have a cup of hot lemon and honey and get into bed.

I am thinking that I have done alright today. Another November 8th finished and I'm OK.

This year, as there was basically naff all we could do, I acknowledge Dusty's birthday with a family walk. Adam was home for the full day, as there's nowhere open to DJ, and we have an early night and no tears.

Adam's DJing had come to an abrupt halt due to lockdown. He was booked for festivals throughout the year, a dream come true for him. He isn't like me though, thinking of a hundred ideas, procrastinating about them for six months, eventually deciding on one idea, taking a course on how to do said idea (although I probably could save myself £200 and work it out for myself), then procrastinating for a further three months, trying to find the confidence to do said idea. He just does it.

He started with listening parties on Twitter, which I couldn't get my head around. Basically it's a group of people, sat in their own front rooms, playing the same album and all talking about it on Twitter. I think that's the gist of it. I switched off when Adam was telling me. Not my kind of party.

He then decided he wanted to do a podcast so he just **did it**!! I know, how weird!

I'd love to be more like Adam in that sense (not the parties for one sense – they're not really really the kind of parties I'd like to attend).

He practised on a few recordings and played them to me to see what I thought. His opening words were "Yo yo yo." " Hmmm, I'm not sure about that, Adam. It does sort of remind me of Jimmy Saville, and correct me if I'm wrong, that's not the vibe you're going for?"

He changed it.

He's gone on to make over thirty podcasts now. If you're into your indie music then give them a listen. They're called *Listen Up Music* and definitely won't remind you of Jimmy Saville.

THINGS I AM GRATEFUL FOR IN 2020:

• Having big boobs to bounce back up if I fall whilst running.

• I've managed to stop looking at Adam and seeing Jimmy Saville.

• Having an uneventful and relaxing day for Dusty's birthday this year.

SELF-HELP TIP

Self belief

If you'd have said self-belief to me a few years ago, I would have thought you were talking a load of mumbo jumbo, and you probably have hairy armpits. To be honest, hey, don't we all in lockdown!

But as I'm now being open to new things, it's something I've researched a lot.

We believe in others but why do we find it so difficult to believe in ourselves? Adam told me he was doing a podcast and I didn't automatically think of what could go wrong. I believed in him.

Self-belief is your belief in your own ability to succeed, having faith in your own capabilities. When you believe in yourself, you can overcome self-doubt and have the confidence to reach for your goals. I'm not talking about cockiness and arrogance, that's different, but there's no reason why you shouldn't believe in yourself.

Decide what it is you want to do. List (you know I love a list) all the reasons you think you can't do this and go through each one. I bet if you really looked at the reasons you think you can't do something, it will be because twenty years ago someone said something negative about it or you took it as a negative. They probably won't even remember saying it, but it's affecting the way you live your life twenty years later. Draw a line under it, write it down and throw that shit away.

We all have strengths and weaknesses. We can't all be great at everything. So write another list of your strengths and just focus on those. When you focus on your strengths you will effortlessly feel more competent and confident. Once you get belief in your strengths, it will have a knock-on effect to those things that you think are your weaknesses.

It's not
who you are
THAT HOLDS YOU BACK,
IT'S WHO YOU THINK
YOU'RE NOT.

December

December sort of crept up on us. I don't know why as there was rock all else to do. I had thankfully remembered to get the elves out of the attic but completely forgotten advent calendars. I messaged Adam (as he was on a late shift) to collect two calendars on his way home. I'm sure he was well chuffed going to three supermarkets at midnight on November 30th. Suffice to say he failed in his mission and came home with two chocolate Father Christmases. I had to convince the Stinks that advent calendars were so last year.

We haven't really done the 'elf on the shelf' thing properly before, but I gathered as this year had been a bit of a flop we'd go all out. When I say 'we', I obviously mean me. When I was on elf duty, the elves would be having nerf gun fights, writing 'poo' on the walls in chocolate spread, sat on the toilet with poo (chocolate spread) smeared all over the seat. (Poo is always a winner in our house.) When Adam was on elf duty, they put their heads in the biscuit tin. Yeah, great Adam.

I'm sure it's not just me that has told the kids the elves have gone back to the North Pole only to be found in Mummy's wardrobe two weeks later. Those pesky elves!

This year wasn't as stressful with school either. Usually there is a newsletter which comes out mid-November that you need a personal assistant to help with the planning and preparation. You needed to remember which day they need to wear their Christmas jumpers and which day was odd sock days, which days they needed to take a gift in and so on. We only had a couple of socially distanced carol singing afternoons we needed to attend this year, so it was pretty stress free.

A couple of years back, when Albie was in playschool, he was dressed as a king for his nativity play and they had to sing *Little Donkey*. They must have been told to sing loudly by the teachers. We were sat down, waiting to catch a glimpse or hear Albie singing, and as soon as they started all we could hear were Albie's dulcet tones. I couldn't stop laughing. He was clueless about how loud he was singing and seemed so proud of himself. Even one of the other kings shouted "be quiet" but that didn't deter him. Due to this past experience, I was excited to see him in his first nativity play at school.

Whilst waiting for the school nativity, all the parents and grandparents get there ridiculously early and stand at the school reception, laughing and chatting, making small talk, whilst keeping one eye firmly on the hall doors. Let's not be coy here, we all want the best seats and the small talk is just a ploy to keep everyone else distracted. As soon as that hall door opens it really is every man for themselves.

I impressed myself as this time I managed to get a seat on the front row. High five, Irene. Thankfully my heavy breathing had subsided by the time the children came into the hall.

Albie saw me and proceeded to turn his back to me and put his finger up his nose. Are you effin' joking, Albie? I have rugby tackled Bethany's mum and side-elbowed Frankie's grandma in the ribs to get this seat and you won't even look at me, never mind sing.

Ted made up for it. Although I didn't manage to get front row seats at his last nativity, I had a full view at the end when all the children were bowing and the parents cheered and whooped. I saw Ted (dressed as Father Christmas) turn his back ready to pull a moonie. It was like it was in slow motion. My God, no child!!! Thankfully, he was doing this to wind me up, but I think all the teachers were ready to do a smack down too.

I tend to start Christmas shopping early. I have a list – of course I do. I have a budget too but that all goes tits up in December. I'd already lost things bought in October and put in a safe place. Where the hell is that fitted bed sheet that I made Ted put on his Christmas list?

As I'm shite with budgets, to get the Stinks money savvy I told them they could earn some money so they could buy their own presents this year. We worked out what jobs earnt them what amount of money and they were eager to earn as much as possible. (Winning at this parenting lark, Irene.) It wasn't until ten past five the next morning – when I thought we were being burgled, but on investigating realised it was Albie tidying his bedroom for 20 pence – that I started to consider that maybe I wasn't winning as much as I thought in the parenting game. It was then that it occurred to me that I needed to put some rules in place surrounding their earning.

This year, more than ever, most of my shopping was done online. It takes some of the joy out of it. I love having a day off work before Christmas and shopping till I drop. To be fair, it doesn't even have to be Christmas. I just love shopping anytime of the year.

Clothing stores were advertising Christmas party dresses. Are they having a laugh? And everywhere I looked there were 'shackets' being sold. Shacket? What the hell is that word? It reminds me of the word 'smegma' (I just wanted to write that one last time). Words like this should be banned. Just call it a shirt/jacket.

People everywhere were hanging on Boris' every word, hoping and praying we could all get together at least for Christmas day.

I had bought Christmas cards for the Stinks as they insisted on sending them. I had stopped a long time ago. This was the first year Albie had written his own. His first card started with:

To Leo,
Hi, I hope you have a good Christmas,
Happy Christmas
Love from Albie
xxx

That's a bloody blog in my eyes! Needless to say, we only managed one card that way and towards the end he just wrote 'Albie x', and not even the recipient's name.

NOREEN'S STORY
They are always children in your eyes*

My daughter was the sort of child that every year searched high and low for Christmas presents before Christmas Day. I had to get more and more imaginative each year when hiding presents.

When she was twenty-six (yes twenty-six!) I had bought her a coat she had pointed out 'in passing' as something she would love. As she had now left home, I didn't think about hiding coat, and the day I bought it I left it hung up on the wardrobe ready to wrap.

It wasn't till the next day when I was in work and got a call from my daughter saying she was going to nip over to my house to collect something that I suddenly thought, 'Oh my God, the coat is hung up in the bedroom.'

I immediately told my boss the situation and explained I needed to get home and move the coat. My boss quite rightly queried wasn't my daughter twenty-six? I told her that didn't matter, she would still search the house for Christmas presents if she got the chance.

Thankfully, my manager saw the urgency and let me nip home. I managed to move the coat before my daughter saw it and on Christmas Day she was surprised and elated with the gift.

Later, we all watched *Coronation Street* together, the Christmas special. Our faces dropped when Rita Fairclough walked into the Rovers Return wearing the exact same coat.

The coat was returned Boxing Day.

*Irene: The daughter was me!

Remember my awards nominations, well one had been cancelled and the other one was going ahead virtually. I was excited, although I would have rather it had been in person.

A few years back when I was heavily pregnant with Albie, Adam had been nominated for a couple of awards at work. It was exciting. I borrowed a formal maternity dress, squeezed myself into it and tried to contour my double chins, adding a couple of contouring lines on my chubby arms to finish the look. When we arrived, each person had a bag of freebies on their seat. You know how much I love free stuff. All the people around our table were nominated for the same awards, which was a bit awkward. When it came to Adam's award, I knew he was going to win it, so much so, I moved my bag of freebies out of the way so he wouldn't trip on the way to collect his award. Adam's name was called out as the winner. He stood up whilst everyone clapped and turned to hug his female boss to the right of him. Ahem!!! I wish I'd left the freebie bag in his way now and filmed him tripping up so I could put it on social media. Your WIFE is right here, Adam! All joking aside, I was so proud of him, even if he didn't hug his chubby, heavily pregnant wife first.

I wanted that experience too, but it wasn't to be. I did my hair, put some makeup on (big effort these days) and got a nice top out to wear – no point in taking my pyjama bottoms off. I logged into the awards. After all that, I wasn't even on camera. I wanted to win, I'm not going to lie. The Stinks were TikToking around me, Adam was late home from work. Not the experience I had imagined. Regardless, positive thinking Irene, positive thinking. And guess what? I didn't win. Oh well, at least my acceptance speech can be saved for the next time! I seem to be collecting unused acceptance speeches.

Here's my list of what to include when I eventually have something to accept.

THANK YOU TO:

- The Stinks for being ~~naughty~~ highly spirited kids, giving me the material to write about.
- To Mr Lycra for inventing stretchy material. You have been a lifesaver this year.
- Mrs Designer for designing me this glamourous tent as it's the only thing that fits me.
- My readers who thank Christ they do not have my life.
- Mr Director who made my book into a hit TV show and got me my open plan kitchen.
- Oh, and my husband, Adam, thanks for your surname.

I'd like to say I was grown up about it and lost gallantly, but I didn't. I shouted at the Stinks for making so much noise and I was in a mood with Adam for being late home. However, he did bring chocolate home so I did mellow a little bit.

LIZ'S STORY
Everyone's a critic!

I had a very important Zoom meeting that I thought I should make an effort for. So I donned some clothes as opposed to pyjamas and put some makeup on.

On collecting Spud from school, he looked at me intently as asked, "Why do you look all makeup-y?" I explained to him that I wanted to look smart as I had been on a Zoom meeting.

He then went on to say, "Your face is the colour of raw spaghetti!"

Great, thanks Spud, that was shade I was going for.

So as a little pick-me-up, I did one of my favourite things and ordered my new planner for the year ahead. I had big plans for 2021 (déjà vu). A lot of research goes into ordering a new planner. I ordered one for Hannah too. I don't bother with Catherine as she wouldn't use a planner, she's more of a 'fly by the seat of her pants' kinda person so it would be wasted on her.

Boris had said the words that everyone had wanted to hear: we could spend Christmas Day together. Whoop whoop.

I was so excited just to spend time as a family. My Christmas budget had been blown out of the water but all my gifts were purchased. I just had to find where I'd hid them now. I think after a year like we've all had, you appreciate the small things even more. I wasn't sure if Boris had addressed the hugging situation but I would be hugging all Christmas Day.

I think Boris' announcement gave everyone a lift and something to look forward to. I booked a drive-through cinema ticket for Christmas Eve where we would be watching *The Polar Express* and eating copious amounts of shite at 9.30 in the morning.

As things were looking up, I decided I was going to up my game and have a website created, and have professional photos taken to go on it. I was going to invest in myself. I was on fire. I believed I could achieve and that's half the battle, right? This book was well on its way. I had started to create my own planners, thinking as I do so much research into the damn things I may as well create one for myself. (obviously I have procrastinated about this for months first). I planned a marketing strategy as opposed to winging it. Check me out. I was going to be creating lots more content to go on my social media and was going to be more consistent. Consistency is not something that comes naturally. Anything that I'm still achieving after three week in is a win in my eyes.

So on Wednesday, 23rd December, I made my big announcement on social media about what I had planned for the New Year, about how I was going to take over the world, and my plans for writing and creating planners. I say big announcement, but it was probably only my mum and my sisters watching.

About an hour later, my mum and dad popped round to tell me the news that my dad had been diagnosed with lung cancer that afternoon.

Devastated doesn't quite cut it. They had spent the lockdown making sure they kept safe and getting in their exercise daily and the enemy was already growing inside my dad. My initial reaction was, right, let's do this. What's the plan? When we can get it out? Let's make a list of who we need to contact. The frustrating thing was it was Christmas time and most people were shutting down for two weeks and organisations were reduced to skeleton staff. So there wasn't a plan. There wasn't anything.

Cancer is something, thankfully, we haven't had to deal with as a family before. You hear about people being diagnosed all the time and within a few months they're ringing that bell.

You don't hear about the pain someone is in every minute of the day and night. But seeing someone you love who is in pain like that is heartbreaking. You would do anything to stop it for them but you are helpless.

My dad's cancer is called a Pancoast tumour and is described as one of the most painful, aggressive ones there is. Why couldn't he have a good tumour like Brian? Brian was the best out of a bad bunch. We knew how to deal with knobheads like Brian. We haven't given Dad's tumour a name, we're not at that stage yet, but when it is gone we will find the vilest and most appropriate name for it.

Christmas Eve arrived and we went to the drive-through cinema with the Stinks as planned and tried to just enjoy the moment with them. Halfway through, a violinist dressed in tin foil got on the stage and played Christmas songs. I'm not sure where the relevance of the tin foil came into it, but the Stinks loved it. It was a lovely family moment. I had Ted on my knee and Albie was on Adam's and we were all singing songs top note. The violinist went on to play The Pogues' *Fairy Tale in New York* – well, that set me off. This is my dad's favourite Christmas song. As I sang on top note there were tears streaming down my cheeks. Adam took my hand and squeezed it and we all sang louder through tears and snot, looking like a car full of not rights. Luckily, the Stinks were so engrossed, they hadn't a clue about the blubbing mess behind them.

Christmas Day was bittersweet. We tried to make the best of it and we did hug a lot but we all knew there was this big nasty unrelenting alien lurking in the room with us and there was F*** all we could do about it. I never told the Stinks. I didn't want to worry them and wanted to keep Christmas as normal as possible for them.

My dad turned from a man who strutted his stuff, still with his swagger as he walked down the street, to a frail old man overnight without any warning. This wasn't how it was supposed to be. We all spent our evenings searching online for success stories, new therapies, anything we could share amongst us as a positive story.

My dad's cancer is not operable but he can have treatment to try and shrink it, so at least we have some hope. That is all everyone has had this year, hope.

So even though 2021 isn't going to be the year I had imagined (again). I know I have some tools to get me through it. Tools that will help me keep my head, so I can help my mum keep hers, and in turn, along with my sisters, we will get my dad get through this.

THINGS I AM GRATEFUL FOR IN 2020:

HOPE

LOOK FOR THE

effin'

Rainbows!

Epilogue

Now you know what 2020 was like for me – a year like no other for all of us.

My dad has had some radiotherapy treatment and is responding well. We are slowly seeing glimpse of the man he used to be at the start of 2020, a grumpy arse with a swagger.

He has had to go to the Christie hospital daily, and they have been amazing. One particular day, my mum dropped him off at the entrance and told him to wait inside for her "but don't forget to wash your hands before you go in", as she went off to find a parking space.

On getting back to the hospital, my dad explained how he had washed his hands with a bottle of water sat on a table at the entrance only to be told off by the hospital security guard as that was his bottle of water for drinking. But other than that, it all went as well as we could have hoped for. Time will tell.

The Stinks are still the Stinks, we have daily fights, daily tears and daily laughter and I cherish that.

I hope you have enjoyed reading the stories from my friends and don't report the lot of us to social services. I'm not sure Bolton social services have the capacity to deal with all of us.

I am looking forward to seeing what you think about this book. Hopefully it will have helped you in some way. I have written about all the tools I have used throughout the year and know they won't suit everyone. But there may be just that one thing in here that will help find your rainbows.

My plans are now to create planners and journals which go alongside this book, so no flowers and fluffiness, more like swearing and attitude. I'm not sure if there will be a book three, although menopause and moody teenagers stories spring to mind. Overall, my plan is to enjoy the life I have and make the most out of every day. Even those days I need to do jack shit because we all need days like that too.

Whilst I'm still bragging about my most improved player trophy and having not received any more awards to add to the list, I know this year has been a year of learning. Learning to improve myself. There's still so much I have to learn, as Adam will confirm. I've not got my shit together 100% of the time. Pffft, but who has? However, I've still got my acceptance speeches ready for when I *do* get my BAFTA award and I will continue to look for dresses. So watch this space.

Adam is looking forward to DJing at festivals this year and his podcast is doing well, now we have deleted the Jimmy Saville elements to it. Check him out on social media platforms, 'Listen Up Music', and tell him Irene sent you. Although, if you're anything like me, he sadly won't be playing Wet Wet Wet or Spice Girls. He's too cool for that apparently.

I would love to hear your funny stories of 2020. If we can get through this year, we can get through anything. If you enjoyed this book, please could you take a moment to leave me a review on any book selling site. If you would like to give me some negative/constructive feedback, please contact me on my telephone number: 1234567890. If there's no answer, just leave a message!

You can contact me via all social media platforms and my website **www.lookforrainbows.com.** I will also be adding more of my ramblings to the blog section on there.

And remember, if the shit hits the fan:

About the Author

Irene Wignall is a new author who only attempted writing when she realised her head was full of randomness and she needed to offload some of it. When Irene started writing she was dealing with some very big events in her life and writing became like having a counselling session without the cost. The reactions to Irene's first book, Look for the effin Rainbows spurred Irene on to continue writing.

"I realised people like to read about real people, not the highlights you see on social media. It helps them feel good about their own lives, and who doesn't want that?"

Irene is a full-time detective in the police, an amazing mum, an amazing wife, and obviously writing this herself.

She is 45 years old and lives in Bolton with her family.

Irene's hobbies include writing (obviously), attempting to run and eating. The latter is something Irene has excelled in during 2020.

Acknowledgments

I would like to say a massive thank you to those of you who shared your stories. You helped me with my anxiety, thinking it wasn't just me who cocked up in life.

A big thanks to Emma, Mo and Laura, who told their very honest and heartbreaking stories. It means a lot to me. Emma is winning at life and smashing the life insurance industry. That's a sentence I could never imagine writing before. Laura is still smashing being tee total and helping others along the way, and Mo has turned her life around dramatically and is a volunteer for a well-known alcohol support group and helps Irene promote alcohol awareness at work. Mo hasn't touched alcohol since the day she left the doctors, 14th November 1994. If you check out my website I have added Mo's poem in the blog section which is brilliant if you fancy a read.

A massive thank you to Siân-Elin Flint-Freel, my book mentor. A lady I wish I'd met years ago. Siân understands everything I'm trying to write and helps me put it into words that others can understand – which is helpful when you're writing a book for others to read!

Thank you to my husband, Adam, who is happy to have a crazy wife. A lesser man would be broken.

The biggest thanks goes to the Stinks; without them, I would have nothing to say! Thank you, Ted, Dusty and Albie xxx

Lightning Source UK Ltd.
Milton Keynes UK
UKHW020415150521
383731UK00008B/236